PREFACE

1. Scope

This publication sets forth the joint doctrine for the planning and execution of meteorological and oceanographic operations in support of joint operations throughout the range of military operations.

2. Purpose

This publication has been prepared under the direction of the Chairman of the Joint Chiefs of Staff. It sets forth joint doctrine to govern the activities and performance of the Armed Forces of the United States in joint operations and provides the doctrinal basis for interagency coordination and for US military involvement in multinational operations. It provides military guidance for the exercise of authority by combatant commanders and other joint force commanders and prescribes joint doctrine for operations, education, and training. It provides military guidance for use by the Armed Forces in preparing their appropriate plans. It is not the intent of this publication to restrict the authority of the joint force commander from organizing the force and executing the mission in a manner the joint force commander deems most appropriate to ensure unity of effort in the accomplishment of the overall objective.

3. Application

a. Joint doctrine established in this publication applies to the Joint Staff, commanders of combatant commands, subunified commands, joint task forces, subordinate components of these commands, and the Services.

b. The guidance in this publication is authoritative; as such, this doctrine will be followed except when, in the judgment of the commander, exceptional circumstances dictate otherwise. If conflicts arise between the contents of this publication and the contents of Service publications, this publication will take precedence unless the Chairman of the Joint Chiefs of Staff, normally in coordination with the other members of the Joint Chiefs of Staff, has provided more current and specific guidance. Commanders of forces operating as part of a multinational (alliance or coalition) military command should follow multinational doctrine and procedures ratified by the United States. For doctrine and procedures not ratified by the United States, commanders should evaluate and follow the multinational command's doctrine and procedures, where applicable and consistent with US law, regulations, and doctrine.

For the Chairman of the Joint Chiefs of Staff:

CURTIS M. SCAPARROTTI
Lieutenant General, U.S. Army
Director, Joint Staff

SUMMARY OF CHANGES
REVISION OF JOINT PUBLICATION 3-59
DATED 24 SEPTEMBER 2008

- Updates space weather information and its impacts on operations.

- Eliminates information on weather observations taken by Army intelligence personnel as a nontraditional source of meteorological and oceanographic (METOC) data.

- Updates nontraditional sources of METOC data for the Army to include further information on tactical weather data.

- Updates nontraditional sources of METOC data for the Navy to include subsurface METOC data and astronomy, geophysics, and precise time.

- Updates Figure III-1, Meteorological and Oceanographic Operations Support Community.

- Establishes a senior meteorological (SMO) and joint meteorological and oceanographic officer planning checklist.

- Updates information on Marine Corps METOC forces.

- Updates information on special operations component METOC forces.

- Clarifies SMO designation in multinational operations.

- Clarifies SMO designation and relationship between the National Weather Service and Department of Homeland Security as it relates to interagency operations within the United States.

- Establishes a new vignette on METOC during Operation TOMODACHI.

- Establishes a new vignette on METOC in riverine operations.

- Replaces the term "Marine air traffic control squadron" with "Marine air control squadron."

- Replaces the term "civil support" with "defense support of civil authorities."

- Removes "chemical, biological, radiological, nuclear, and high yield explosives" as a term.

- Removes terms previously approved for deletion from Joint Publication (JP) 1-02.

- Removes mention of specific references in Appendix E.

- Establishes appendix, "Meteorological and Oceanographic Integration to Joint Special Operations Planning."

- Updates appendix on references.

TABLE OF CONTENTS

Page

CHAPTER V
EXECUTION OF METEOROLOGICAL AND OCEANOGRAPHIC OPERATIONS

APPENDIX

GLOSSARY

FIGURE

EXECUTIVE SUMMARY
COMMANDER'S OVERVIEW

- **Provides an overview of the key functions and principles of meteorological and oceanographic (METOC) operations**

- **Describes METOC characterization of the environment, environmental exploitation, and nontraditional sources of METOC data**

- **Addresses roles and responsibilities of METOC forces**

- **Explains METOC operations in joint operation planning**

- **Covers execution of METOC operations**

Introduction

Joint meteorological and oceanographic (METOC) operations are critical to a commander's awareness of the operational environment and the ability to exploit that awareness to gain an advantage during military operations.

Meteorological and oceanographic (METOC) forces work cooperatively within the Department of Defense community and across interorganizational lines to share and obtain information to provide timely, accurate, relevant, and consistent METOC support to joint force commanders (JFCs). METOC examines the whole range of atmospheric (weather) and oceanographic phenomena, from the sub-bottom of the Earth's oceans up to the top of the atmosphere and the space environment (space weather).

Understanding METOC Terminology

METOC is a term used to convey all meteorological, oceanographic, and space environmental factors as provided by the Services, support agencies, and other sources. These factors include the whole range of atmospheric (weather) and oceanographic phenomena, from the sub-bottom of the Earth's oceans up to the top of the atmosphere and the space environment (space weather).

METOC Key Functions

Joint METOC operations focus on two key functions: characterization of the environment and exploitation of environmental information to gain an operational advantage and ensure the safety of operational forces.

METOC Principles

The principles of accuracy, consistency, relevancy, and timeliness are the cornerstone of joint METOC operations. When characterizing the environment, the principles of accuracy and consistency are paramount to collection, analysis, and prediction processes. The guiding principles of relevancy and timeliness are critical in tailoring and integrating METOC products for the commander.

Meteorological and Oceanographic Operations

Characterization of the Environment

METOC operations depend on continuous characterization of the environment, which includes:

- **Collection.** METOC personnel collect environmental measurements from air, land, maritime, and space, using on-site and remote sensing platforms.

- **Analysis.** METOC production facilities, reachback centers, and on-scene METOC personnel interpret, fuse, and evaluate collected data and information to develop forecasts and recommendations in support of operational requirements and decisions.

- **Prediction.** Through the use of numerical models, expert systems, and human judgment, METOC forces describe the anticipated future state of the meteorological, oceanographic, and space environment. Forecasts, computer and human based, include temporal and spatial assessments of atmospheric, terrestrial, marine, and space environmental features and associated elements.

Environmental Exploitation

Environmental exploitation is composed of two processes: tailoring predicted data to meet specific operational requirements and integrating the tailored forecast into operation planning and execution. METOC forces tailor information into mission execution and planning forecast products by applying METOC parameter thresholds specific to a mission, platform, or system. Integration of METOC information into planning and decision-making processes allows the JFC to optimize weapons, sensors, platforms, mission profiles, tactics, techniques and procedures, and personnel while marginalizing the benefit of the environment for the adversary, thereby creating an asymmetrical advantage.

Tailored Products

A key role of METOC forces is to support the decision-making process of the JFC and assigned forces through application of forecast products tailored to their operational requirements. METOC forces tailor information into actionable decision aid and mission execution/planning forecast products often by applying METOC parameter thresholds specific to a mission, platform, or system.

Integration

Effective integration means getting accurate, consistent, relevant, and timely information to the appropriate decision authority to anticipate, exploit, and mitigate any METOC conditions that may impact operations.

Integration of METOC information into planning and decision-making processes allows the JFC and assigned forces to optimize the employment of military capabilities while marginalizing the benefit of the environment for the adversary, thereby creating an asymmetrical advantage for friendly forces. Effective integration of METOC information aids the planning of joint military operations and enables commanders to anticipate and then mitigate or exploit environmental impacts on planned operations.

Nontraditional Sources of METOC Data

Nontraditional METOC data can be gathered from diverse Department of Defense manned organic units, unmanned systems, and from various intelligence sensor bases. These additional data are critical to supplementing the METOC database from which the various METOC echelons derive analysis and forecast products. Examples of nontraditional sources for METOC data include: reconnaissance units, operating forces, surface ships, and aircrews.

Meteorological and Oceanographic Forces

METOC Organizations and Staffs

The geographic combatant commander (GCC) provides guidance and is responsible for the direction of METOC assets within the area of responsibility (AOR). In some cases, the GCC may designate the senior meteorological and oceanographic officer (SMO) to also function as the joint meteorological and oceanographic officer (JMO). The appointment of JMOs should align with the combatant command's (CCMD's) METOC concept of operations.

Senior Meteorological and Oceanographic Officer

Each combatant commander (CCDR) may designate a SMO to coordinate all METOC operations within the AOR or functional responsibility. The SMO interacts with the CCDR's staff, the CCMD's components, assigned and attached METOC units, other CCMD SMOs, and other agencies to ensure unity of effort.

Joint Meteorological and Oceanographic Officer

The JMO supports all aspects of planning, deployment and employment. The JMO interacts with the staff components, regional and partner nation (North Atlantic Treaty Organization) METOC units, and the SMO to optimize METOC operations.

Meteorological and Oceanographic Operations Support Community and Joint Meteorological and Oceanographic Coordination Organization

The **meteorological and oceanographic operations support community** (MOSC) includes (but would not be limited to) METOC forecast centers, oceanographic teams, and operational weather squadrons. METOC personnel assigned to a joint task force (JTF) will not normally be sufficient to provide autonomous staff support without reachback to the MOSC. The SMO or JMO can recommend one unit as the **joint METOC coordination organization** to support a particular JTF and to coordinate all other MOSC units to provide products and services to the joint force.

Service and Functional Component METOC Forces

Component METOC officers provide recommendations to their commanders and serve as the focal point for component METOC planning and execution.

Army

Artillery meteorological sections use a suite of meteorological sensors and large-scale atmospheric data from the Air Force Weather Agency (AFWA) to produce a vertical profile of wind speed and direction, temperature, relative humidity, cloud base height, type precipitation, and horizontal visibility in the target area, all of which are necessary for precise targeting and terminal guidance of various munitions.

Marine Corps

Marine Corps METOC is organized as an embedded capability set within selected Marine Corps units (e.g., Marine air control squadrons, intelligence battalions) to support military operations in both garrison and tactical environments.

Navy

Navy METOC personnel provide data collection, assimilation capabilities, products, and services to operating forces ashore and afloat, which are tailored according to the requirements of the component, individual numbered fleet, and task force commanders.

Air Force

Air Force METOC forces also provide direct and general support to the Army forces (ARFOR) and supported echelons. The Air Force provides METOC capabilities to the ARFOR in a direct and general support role as part of the Air Force forces. The AFWA and subordinate organizations provide general support in the form of global forecasting, climatological services, and collection and dissemination of satellite data.

Special Operation Forces

Special operations forces (SOF) METOC forces provide METOC operations and tailored services/support to SOF command and control elements, SOF aviation assets, the joint special operations air component, and subordinate organizations.

Meteorological and Oceanographic Operations in Joint Operational Planning

METOC support includes integrating global, regional, and locally produced METOC products as well as data and products received from supporting agencies and reliable indigenous sources.

The size, structure, and content of METOC operations depends on the JFC's operational needs. The SMO incorporates this assessment into a comprehensive sensing strategy and includes it in applicable theater plans. The study and application of historical METOC data/information is invaluable for planning, staging, and executing joint operations and for providing the initial basis for a METOC collection plan.

METOC Operations in Joint Operation Planning

The Joint Operation Planning and Execution System is the primary system for military operation planning and execution, including requests for forces. SMOs/JMOs ensure appropriate METOC support is provided or requested for joint forces. METOC support is critical to the joint operational planning process. Exploiting this information allows the warfighter to take advantage of METOC conditions and minimize impacts of adverse conditions. The SMO/JMO must completely understand the assigned mission and provide tailored products during each step of the joint operation planning process to ensure success.

Execution of Meteorological and Oceanographic Operations

General

METOC support normally begins well prior to force deployment and often ends after redeployment of the joint force is complete. METOC forces, databases, products, and equipment must be responsive to the requirements of the JFC and should be maintained to a degree of readiness that ensures immediate employment capability.

Deployment

The SMO and JMO should provide or arrange METOC operations and support to these phases as outlined:

- **Deployment Planning.** Advise the JFC of climatological factors that could potentially hamper force deployment.

- **Predeployment Activities.** Advise the JFC of METOC conditions that could hamper force embarkation, transit, and force debarkation.

- **Movement.** Continue to advise the JFC of METOC conditions that could hamper force embarkation, transit, and force debarkation.

- **Joint Reception, Staging, Onward Movement, and Integration (JRSOI).** As JRSOI actions decrease, the SMO and JMO's focus should turn to theater and force employment.

Employment

The rapidly changing nature of the air, land, maritime, and space domains makes METOC data extremely perishable. **Communication of METOC information** should be designed to fulfill the data collection, storage, retrieval, and dissemination efforts of the METOC forces at all levels. The **joint meteorological and oceanographic coordination cell** (JMCC) synchronizes and integrates all METOC information for the JFC's operational area. The task of the JMCC is to combine multiple source METOC information with operational information to generate the joint operational area forecast with a coherent METOC picture.

Redeployment

The JMCC's will focus on port operations during redeployment. The SMO and JMO advise the JFC of environmental features which would hamper the redeployment process.

CONCLUSION

This publication provides doctrine for planning, coordinating, and conducting joint meteorological and oceanographic operations.

Intentionally Blank

CHAPTER I
INTRODUCTION

"Know yourself, know your enemy; Your victory will never be endangered. Know the ground, know the weather; Your victory will then be total…"

Sun Tzu, Chinese General, 500 B.C.

1. Overview

a. Joint meteorological and oceanographic (METOC) operations are critical to a commander's awareness of the operational environment and the ability to exploit that awareness to gain an advantage during military operations. Few military endeavors, including those of our adversaries, are immune to the effects of the natural environment. Neglected or ignored, the natural environment and its effects can negatively impact even the most carefully planned and executed campaigns and operations. Properly applied, joint METOC operations can provide our air, land, maritime, space, and special operations forces (SOF) with a significant, even decisive, advantage over our enemies.

b. METOC forces work cooperatively within the Department of Defense (DOD) community and across interorganizational lines to share and obtain information to provide

ONE OPERATION, ONE FORECAST

Every forecaster has their own calculus, and it is a rare day when two or more can completely agree on a forecast. But coordinating military actions within a theater requires a coordinated METOC (meteorological and oceanographic) view. This need is expressed in joint METOC by the phrase "One Operation, One Forecast." At no time was this more evident than during the planning for the Allied assault in Normandy that was Operation OVERLORD.

"June 4, 1944. Group Captain J. M. Stagg of the RAF (Royal Air Force) must provide Ike with the final piece of information he needs to launch OVERLORD – one that no one could control or keep secret. What will the weather be like on D-Day?

To help him answer that crucial question, Stagg had six different weather services (American and British land, sea, and air) feeding him information. On the morning of June 4, to his dismay, he had six distinct weather predictions to pick from… He made up his own prediction, one that drew upon all the others but was uniquely his. Despite the intense storm of June 4, Stagg predicted a break in the weather for June 6. Ike trusted his source. He decided to take the risk and go."

Stephen Ambrose and Richard Immerman
Ike's Spies: Eisenhower and the Espionage Establishment, 1999

timely, accurate, relevant, and consistent METOC support to joint force commanders (JFCs) and their component forces. The lines of responsibility and authority for the collection and production of METOC information are sometimes blurred. It is imperative that joint METOC personnel participate in the planning process and in various boards, cells, and working groups to address specific issues and maintain situational awareness. This also facilitates a "one operation, one forecast" approach.

c. This publication describes how METOC capabilities should be employed through all phases of joint operations. It describes the capabilities, roles, functions, planning considerations, and integration concepts of each METOC element within the joint force.

2. Understanding Meteorological and Oceanographic Terminology

METOC is a term used to convey all meteorological, oceanographic, and space environmental factors as provided by the Services, support agencies, and other sources. These factors include the whole range of atmospheric (weather) and oceanographic phenomena, from the sub-bottom of the Earth's oceans up to the top of the atmosphere and the space environment (space weather).

a. Atmospheric phenomena include not only conditions at a given point and time, but also long-term climatic averages of conditions and hazards to operations such as volcanic ash, dust or icing/turbulence.

b. Oceanographic phenomena typically include the physical characteristics of the ocean such as waves, tides, and currents. However, from a military perspective, oceanography also includes biological factors (e.g., marine mammals), bathymetry, hydrography, geophysics, and astrometry.

c. Space weather phenomena occur within the space and near-Earth environment and typically originate from solar flares and coronal mass ejections. Highly-charged solar particles impacting the Earth's magnetic field and ionosphere can have negative consequences for military operations. These solar events can degrade terrestrial radio and satellite communications, degrade radar systems, induce electrical anomalies on spacecraft, and pose a radiation hazard to high-altitude flight and space operators. Electrical grid damage or disruptions can occur during the most intense solar storms.

d. For the purposes of this publication, METOC information is treated differently than METOC data. METOC data is manipulated and processed to become METOC information. Human judgment and intelligence then places this METOC information into the specific context of the mission to optimize military decision making and operations.

3. Key Functions

a. A timely, accurate, consistent, and relevant characterization of the atmospheric, maritime, terrestrial, and space environment integrated into operation planning can provide commanders information necessary to anticipate and exploit the best window of opportunity to plan, execute, support, and sustain specific operations. Exploiting METOC information during operational planning and continuing through mission execution helps ensure the optimum employment of sensors, weapons, logistics, equipment, and personnel and is key to successful execution of military operations. Further, since all joint military capabilities can be influenced by the environment, analyzing the METOC impacts based on operationally significant METOC threshold sensitivities is central to the development of the environmental estimate and supports and influences the joint intelligence preparation of the operational environment (JIPOE), the joint operational planning process (JOPP), commander's situational awareness, common operational picture (COP), command and control (C2), and other decision making. Joint METOC operations focus on two key functions (see Figure I-1).

      (1) Characterization of the environment.

      (2) Exploitation of environmental information to gain an operational advantage and ensure the safety of operational forces.

    b. Characterizing the environment consists of three core processes: collecting static and

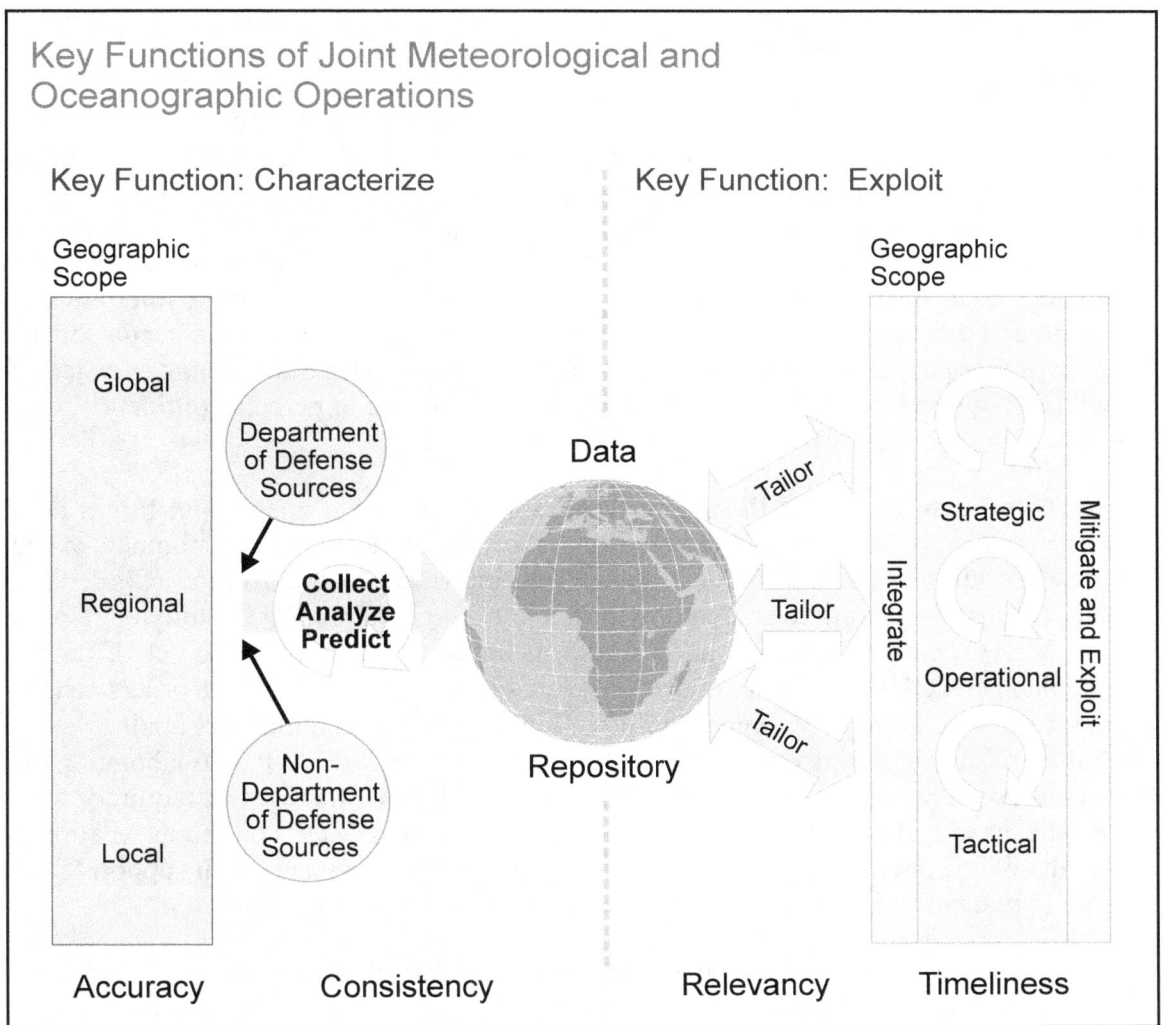

Figure I-1. Key Functions of Joint Meteorological and Oceanographic Operations

dynamic data, analyzing current and past conditions from that data, and predicting future environmental conditions. METOC forces provide critical value by exploiting environmental information through two processes: tailoring information to meet the operational requirements of a particular joint force and integrating this information into the commander's decision-making cycle and C2 systems. Each of these processes is described in greater detail in Chapter II, "Meteorological and Oceanographic Operations."

4. Meteorological and Oceanographic Principles

a. **General.** The principles of accuracy, consistency, relevancy, and timeliness are the cornerstone of joint METOC operations. By applying these principles, METOC forces are better prepared to support planning and decision making. When characterizing the environment, the principles of accuracy and consistency are paramount to collection, analysis, and prediction processes. The guiding principles of relevancy and timeliness are critical in tailoring and integrating METOC products for the commander.

b. **Accuracy.** METOC information must be measurably correct, convey an appreciation of the environment and the conditions as they actually exist, and predict the best possible forecast of future environmental conditions and impacts based on sound judgment. Joint forces depend on accurate METOC information to plan and direct their operations. Inaccurate information can cost lives, undermine the successful execution of a mission, unnecessarily expend resources, and impair readiness. All of the following affect the accuracy of METOC information: the capability to collect data within the area of interest (AOI) with sufficient spatial and temporal coverage to provide situational awareness and to model and forecast the METOC conditions; limitations of METOC data collection equipment and instrumentation; limitations of numerical modeling of the physical environment; the perishable nature of METOC data; and human error. It is essential that the joint meteorological and oceanographic officer (JMO) provides the most accurate predictions of METOC impacts and clearly articulate limits of confidence or percent confidence so the JFC can make the best decision.

c. **Consistency.** Joint METOC operations should provide operational forces at all echelons with consistent information regarding the state of the natural environment, as per the "one operation, one forecast" concept. METOC information supporting a JFC's decision usually comes from multiple sources. Within a joint force there must be unity of effort to ensure METOC forces produce, access, and incorporate the same basic set of data in developing METOC products applied at global, regional, and local levels, in order to ensure similar results. Natural environment information provided to commanders at all echelons should therefore be spatially and temporally consistent across the AOI. Collaboration and coordination between functional and component METOC forces are required when supporting any level of joint operations and especially when METOC conditions will impact the ability of one operational unit to support a larger operation (e.g., close air support [CAS] to ground maneuver forces, carrier air wing support to littoral operations).

d. **Relevancy.** This principle requires the joint force users to communicate their specific requirements for content, form, medium, presentation, timeliness, and frequency of delivery, and asks METOC personnel to satisfy these requirements. It influences the joint force's current, planned, and alternative courses of action (COAs) at each level of responsibility. Each operation requires tailored METOC information so the user can quickly identify and apply relevant information without additional analysis or manipulation. It is also important that the METOC collections, analyses, and predictions provide value to the particular operation for which they are provided.

e. **Timeliness.** METOC operations are only effective when the combatant commander (CCDR) and subordinate JFCs, as well as functional or Service component commanders, receive accurate METOC information in time to consider its impact and apply it effectively within their decision-making cycle. METOC forces must also provide the latest available METOC information and knowledge to decision makers throughout the decision cycle and all phases of joint operations. Reliable communication links among all METOC forces are required to support and sustain the timely dissemination of METOC information and are essential to the overall capability of METOC forces.

METEOROLOGICAL AND OCEANOGRAPHIC PRINCIPLES

Accuracy: Condition of being true, correct, or exact.

Consistency: The attribute of incorporating information from the same, jointly-accepted, spatial and temporal sources.

Relevancy: The attribute of data and information whose significance is quickly identified and applied without additional analysis or manipulation.

Timeliness: The attribute of conveying representative data and information at opportune moments to influence the decision-making process.

METEOROLOGICAL AND OCEANOGRAPHIC PROCESSES

Collect: To sense, acquire, and observe meteorological, oceanographic, and space environmental data.

Analyze: To transform meteorological, oceanographic and space environmental data into information.

Predict: To describe the anticipated future state of the meteorological, oceanographic and space environment.

Tailor: To derive relevant information from environmental parameters for decision making.

Integrate: To enable decision makers to anticipate environmental impacts on planned operations, and then mitigate or exploit those conditions.

Intentionally Blank

CHAPTER II
METEOROLOGICAL AND OCEANOGRAPHIC OPERATIONS

"It is not enough to just understand and predict the air-ocean environment. We must transform that understanding into knowledge of how that environment will impact our sensors, platforms, and people, and communicate the opportunities and constraints afforded by the environment."

Rear Admiral Tim McGee, US Navy
Commander, Naval Meteorology and Oceanography Command, 2006

1. Introduction

This chapter describes the primary functions the METOC community performs, as well as those of nonstandard METOC sources, to support and enhance the full range of joint military operations. METOC operations are actions taken by joint forces to characterize the environment and exploit environmental information.

SECTION A. CHARACTERIZATION OF THE ENVIRONMENT

2. Overview

METOC operations depend on continuous characterization of the environment. METOC data is collected by various sensors and personnel throughout the operational environment, and then analyzed to develop a coherent depiction of the natural environment, which is used to provide situational awareness and to predict the future state of the natural environment. Because of the rapidly changing natural environment, METOC data is perishable and should be continuously collected, analyzed, and disseminated in order to develop accurate predictions.

3. Collection

a. Successful joint operations depend on timely, accurate, and reliable METOC information. METOC personnel collect environmental measurements from air, land, maritime, and space, using on-site and remote sensing platforms. This data populates theater, regional, and global databases from which METOC services and products are produced, providing the foundation for effective METOC operations. During joint operation planning and operations, a sensing strategy and a METOC collection plan must be developed. The sensing strategy leverages all possible instruments of national power to meet the CCDR's ongoing METOC situational awareness requirements and is included in theater plans. It includes organic DOD METOC data collection capabilities and identifies gaps in DOD METOC collection. Non-DOD METOC data also may be available and used if it is determined to be timely, accurate, and reliable to supplement DOD METOC assets and to incorporate into theater METOC processes. The collection plan is developed and implemented to orchestrate the timing, distribution of collection sites, and efforts of all components within the joint force. A complete plan will foster unity of effort while optimizing data collection, dissemination, and integration into METOC products from indigenous and national sources. Spreading observational resources across an AOI to obtain optimum coverage will significantly improve the quality of METOC services. METOC collection plans will normally be published in annex H (Meteorological and Oceanographic Operations) of operation plans (OPLANs)/operation orders (OPORDs).

For additional information on non-DOD METOC data, refer to Chairman of the Joint Chiefs of Staff Instruction (CJCSI) 3810.01C, Meteorological and Oceanographic Operations.

b. Nontraditional collection sources augment standard METOC collection capabilities, particularly in remote or data-sparse AOIs or operations. This information significantly enhances commander's operational battlespace awareness, production center modeling efforts and generation of tailored tactical forecast products. Commanders should emphasize these nontraditional METOC collection efforts throughout an operation because such data may provide the critical, or possibly the only, piece of METOC information pivotal to mission success. Service-specific nontraditional sources of METOC data collectors are summarized in Section C, "Nontraditional Sources of Meteorological and Oceanographic Data."

4. Analysis

METOC production facilities, reachback centers, and on-scene METOC personnel interpret, fuse, and evaluate collected data and information to develop forecasts and recommendations in support of operational requirements and decisions. Analysis products provide coherent, integrated depictions of the past and current state of the natural environment over specific regions. Analysis transforms raw environmental data into useful METOC information and enables production of accurate forecasts of the environment. It enables identification of significant METOC features and conditions, which may require further study and monitoring to determine impacts on operations, based on METOC thresholds and sensitivities, as discussed in paragraph 7, "Tailored Products." METOC information is analyzed and integrated into inputs for decision making.

5. Prediction

a. **Overview.** Through the use of numerical models, expert systems, and human judgment, METOC forces describe the anticipated future state of the meteorological, oceanographic, and space environment. Forecasts, computer and human based, include temporal and spatial assessments of atmospheric, terrestrial, marine, and space environmental features and associated elements.

b. **Numerical Models.** Physics-based simulations of the environment carried out on high-speed computer processors develop solutions of complex mathematical or statistical calculations representing the time evolution of the METOC environment. Various modeling methods provide ranges of certainty and confidence in their characterization of the environment and other earth-system prediction capabilities.

c. **Expert Systems.** Automated problem-solving techniques, which simulate human skill and apply statistical analysis, rapidly post-process METOC parameters in order to provide additional fidelity within the net-centric data repository.

SECTION B. ENVIRONMENTAL EXPLOITATION

6. Overview

Environmental exploitation is composed of two processes: tailoring predicted data to meet specific operational requirements and integrating the tailored forecast into operation planning and execution.

7. Tailored Products

a. **Overview.** A key role of METOC forces is to support the decision-making process of the JFC and assigned forces through application of forecast products tailored to their operational requirements. It is not enough to just understand and predict the air, land, maritime, and space environments, that understanding must be transformed into relevant operational knowledge of how that environment will impact joint operations and military capabilities (weapons, sensors, platforms, mission profiles, tactics, techniques, and procedures [TTP], and personnel).

b. **Operational Support to Decision Makers.** METOC forces tailor information into actionable decision aid and mission execution/planning forecast products often by applying METOC parameter thresholds specific to a mission, platform, or system. Decision makers typically identify these operationally significant METOC threshold sensitivities impacting/affecting the employment of joint operations and military capabilities, providing a baseline for weather effects decision aid rules. Effective tailoring requires METOC personnel to thoroughly understand how the environments of air, land, maritime, and space domains impact operations.

8. Integration

a. **Overview.** Integration of METOC information into planning and decision-making processes allows the JFC and assigned forces to optimize the employment of military capabilities (weapons, sensors, platforms, mission profiles, TTP, and personnel) while marginalizing the benefit of the environment for the adversary, thereby creating an asymmetrical advantage for friendly forces. Effective integration of METOC information aids the planning of joint military operations and enables commanders to anticipate and then mitigate or exploit environmental impacts on planned operations. Commanders should ensure environmental impacts on operations and intelligence are fully integrated into planning and decision-making processes and C2 systems. Continuous coordination between JFC and Service component METOC staffs ensure all available and relevant METOC information and resources, including indigenous assets, are properly considered and made available for use by the joint force.

b. **Requirements.** METOC information directly supports joint operations by identifying METOC effects that influence the JIPOE, JOPP, commander's situational awareness, TTP, C2, weapons, platforms, sensors, and personnel. METOC personnel address METOC-related commander's critical information requirements (CCIRs) and other requirements. They coordinate across staff functions to identify and document applicable critical environmental thresholds to acquire a complete and thorough understanding of METOC impacts to the mission.

OPERATION IRAQI FREEDOM
25-27 MARCH 2003

During the American-led march to Baghdad, meteorological and oceanographic forces predicted the onset of widespread sandstorms in south-central Iraq. Commanders seized the moment and quickly integrated this environmental information into their operational planning. Scheduled missions were modified or cancelled, and new ones were added. Weapons systems vulnerable to the expected conditions were switched out in favor of those that could overcome the degrading effects of persistent strong winds that produced blowing sand and near-zero visibilities up to several thousand feet over the operational area.

Various Sources

---

c. **Communications.** Effective integration means getting accurate, consistent, relevant, and timely information to the appropriate decision authority to anticipate, exploit, and mitigate any METOC conditions that may impact operations. Integration in the joint environment includes evaluation and dissemination of METOC information across all security enclaves and through common architectures and machine-to-machine interfaces. Timeliness is critical to effective integration; therefore, METOC operations rely on robust, assured communications. Environmental information is most effective when it is incorporated early into C2 processes, which allow individual decision makers to fuse relevant METOC impacts with other operational information tailored to their mission.

d. **Feedback.** METOC forces should actively engage with their supported unit and solicit feedback on the timeliness, consistency, accuracy, and relevance of their support. Feedback should be used to improve processes and may drive changes to how support is integrated into joint operations.

SECTION C. NONTRADITIONAL SOURCES OF METEOROLOGICAL AND OCEANOGRAPHIC DATA

9. Summary of Nontraditional Meteorological and Oceanographic Data Sources

a. **Overview.** This section summarizes METOC data available from nontraditional sources (METOC force supplied data is described in Section A, "Characterization of the Environment," and Chapter III, "Meteorological and Oceanographic Forces," paragraph 4, "Service and Functional Component Meteorological and Oceanographic Forces"). Nontraditional METOC data can be gathered from diverse DOD manned organic units, unmanned systems, and from various intelligence sensor bases. These additional data are critical to supplementing the METOC database from which the various METOC echelons derive analysis and forecast products.

"In modern warfare, any single system is easy to overcome; combinations of systems, with each protecting weak points in others and exposing enemy weak points to be exploited by other systems, make for an effective fighting force."

Vice Admiral Stanley R. Arthur
Commander, US Naval Forces, Central Command
Operation DESERT STORM

b. **Army Forces (ARFOR).** The Army has organic resources that provide supplemental reports of METOC conditions. These Army elements possess a limited measuring capability designed to address their own immediate needs and comply with appropriate Army-specific regulations and doctrine. Since Army units are mobile, locations must be included as part of the METOC report; consequently, US classification guides may require these reports to be classified and transmitted over secure communications channels. In addition to the air and space environmental data and information collected by the Air Force, the Army provides for the collection of tactical weather data when deemed necessary. The Army has the capability to collect both full observations and limited parameters or elements. The following represents the most significant sources of weather data within the Army tactical structure.

(1) **Air Traffic Control (ATC) Units.** ATC units may have weather-observing instruments to include measurement of surface pressure, temperature, and surface wind velocity and direction. In addition, aircrews, flight operations personnel, and control tower operators visually estimate horizontal visibility and obstructions to visibility. They also observe such special phenomena as lightning, thunderstorms, and tornadoes. Control tower operators assigned to ATC units should be trained by Air Force METOC personnel to supplement weather situational awareness via the cooperative weather watch process.

(2) **Terrain Analysis Team.** These teams may provide basic stream flow measurements and predictions of river stages and floods.

(3) **Imagery Intelligence Sections.** These sections can provide general information on visibility, cloud cover, trafficability, and flooding, and also offer reachback to intelligence community capabilities that could provide valuable sources of other METOC information.

(4) **Supplemental Weather Observations.** The Services are responsible for collecting weather and environmental data from areas in which the METOC personnel are not manned, trained, or equipped to operate. The Forward Area Limited Observing Program (FALOP) is a battalion or brigade intelligence staff officer (Army; Marine Corps battalion or regiment [S-2]/Army or Marine Corps component intelligence staff officer [G-2]/Navy component intelligence staff officer [N-2]) program under which the S-2/G-2/N-2 and intelligence staff officer personnel collect forward area weather information and transmit the data to US weather personnel.

For additional information on the FALOP program, refer to Army Field Manual (FM) 34-81, Weather Support for Army Tactical Operations.

(5) **Aviation Squadrons and/or Brigades.** Aircrews provide en route or post mission pilot reports (PIREPs). Unmanned aircraft systems (UASs) and observation platforms/balloons may provide sensed data via digital downlink or as deduced by visual imagery.

(6) **Space Support Teams.** The Army obtains some space environmental information from Army space support teams as well as outside sources, such as the Air Force.

(7) **Reconnaissance Units.** Army brigade combat teams (BCTs) have chemical, biological, radiological, and nuclear (CBRN) reconnaissance vehicles that can provide limited meteorological information such as temperature, humidity, wind speed, and wind direction. Army also has long range reconnaissance and surveillance capabilities that can provide meteorological information.

(8) Generally, all company-sized units have a field sanitation team that can provide temperature, wet bulb, and globe temperature readings, as required to monitor heat stress conditions.

(9) **Artillery Meteorological (ARTYMET).** ARTYMET teams provide upper-air observations and artillery limited surface observations in support of artillery units.

c. **Marine Corps Forces (MARFOR).** The Marine Corps has additional non-METOC resources that can provide supplemental METOC condition reports. These Marine Corps elements possess a limited sensing capability designed to meet their specific operational requirements. Consequently, their METOC observing capabilities are supplemental to their primary mission. Since Marine Corps units are expeditionary, locations may be included as part of the METOC report; consequently, Marine Corps observations are normally classified and transmitted over secure communications channels unless otherwise directed. The following represents the most significant sources of METOC data within the Marine Corps' structure.

(1) **Artillery Meteorological.** In general, Marine Corps ARTYMET teams provide upper-air observations and artillery limited surface observations. ARTYMET sections are equipped to perform upper-air observations employing a balloon-sounding method (i.e., rawinsonde and/or pilot balloon).

(2) **Marine Air Control Squadron (MACS).** A MACS has limited weather-observing instruments to include measurement of surface pressure, temperature, and surface wind velocity and direction. In accordance with (IAW) the Navy Meteorology and Oceanography Command Instruction 1500.3, *Procedures for Qualification and Certification of Navy and Marine Corps Air Traffic Controllers as Tower Visibility Observers,* MACS personnel are trained and certified to visually estimate horizontal visibility and obstructions to visibility. Additionally, they can observe and identify such special phenomena as lightning, thunderstorms, and tornadoes. MACS personnel are trained by Marine Corps METOC personnel to provide weather observations for forward operating bases and forward arming and refueling points.

(3) **Reconnaissance Units.** Marine Corps reconnaissance units may provide limited scope METOC observations through intelligence channels. Additionally, reconnaissance units may be tasked through intelligence channels to provide specialized, mission critical observations (e.g., measure ice thickness at a river crossing point).

(4) **Imagery Intelligence Sections.** These sections, when available, can provide imagery information on visibility, cloud cover, battlefield contaminants, and flooding. These sections also offer reachback to intelligence community capabilities that could provide valuable sources of other METOC information.

(5) **Operating Forces.** Some Marine Corps operating forces can provide weather observations. Forces such as intelligence (limited weather observation), counterintelligence (limited weather observation), aviation squadrons (en route and post mission PIREPs), UASs (visual imagery or sensed data via digital downlink), and tank battalions (atmospheric pressure and temperature readings) can provide limited weather observations when requested through appropriate channels from their operational area. As with SOF described in paragraph 9f, "Special Operations Forces," JMOs must be sensitive to operations security (OPSEC) considerations when requesting and incorporating this data into their collection plan.

(6) **Navy Medical Units Assigned to Marine Corps Units.** Per Marine Corps Order 6200.1, *Marine Corps Heat Injury Prevention Program,* wet bulb globe temperature index (WBGTI) readings are required to monitor heat stress conditions. Navy medical units attached to a Marine unit without a Marine Corps METOC section will normally possess and utilize a WBGTI measuring set and can provide temperature, wet bulb, and globe temperature readings.

d. **Navy Forces (NAVFOR)**

(1) **Surface Ships.** All surface combatants, aircraft carriers, and multipurpose amphibious ships provide surface weather observations. Oceanographic depth/temperature profiles are collected when assets are available for launching expendable bathythermographs (BTs) based on operational need and/or prescribed data collection plan.

(2) **Subsurface METOC Data.** Subsurface METOC focuses on oceanographic analysis, bathymetry, and hydrographic mapping. Oceanographic analysis focuses on the tactical aspects of subsurface METOC data, volume and seafloor features, and their variability over the spatial and temporal frame of interest. Bathymetry analysis focuses on natural and man-made features on or near the seafloor. Navy acquires subsurface METOC data from shipboard surveys aboard Military Sealift Command surveying vessels, operational Navy and commercial ships, remotely-sensed data from airborne and satellite sensors, and buoys. Hydrographic surveys, launched from survey ships by fleet survey teams, determine navigational hazards that could impede movement of naval assets.

(3) **Carrier Air Wing and/or Maritime Patrol Aircraft.** Aircrews provide METOC observations as specified by their mission, or when required in areas of sparse data.

BT observations are taken by sonobuoy-equipped aircraft. Generally, a minimum of one BT observation is taken during each antisubmarine warfare flight and/or in data sparse areas.

(4) **Astronomy, Geophysics, and Precise Time.** The United States Naval Observatory (USNO) provides information on astronomy, astronomical applications, earth orientation data, and precise timing. The USNO serves as the official source of time for DOD and a standard of time for the US.

e. **Air Force Forces (AFFOR).** The most significant non-METOC Air Force sources of weather data are aircrews. This is often in the form of PIREPs, Aircraft Communication Addressing and Reporting System reporting, or the information is contained in the target weather and intelligence report. ATC teams have limited observation capabilities. The Air Force also obtains key space and terrestrial environmental information from the Defense Meteorological Satellite Program satellites and the Air Force Weather Agency (AFWA), as well as from outside sources such as universities and research facilities. When available, full motion video from a UAS can also be a significant source of data. AFFOR METOC personnel also maintain situational awareness of environmental events such as volcanoes, earthquakes, and tsunamis using the various regional volcanic ash advisory centers and the US Geological Surveys World Data Center for Seismology, respectively. Webcams, news reports, and government sources indigenous to each region of the globe can be excellent sources of volcanic ash, earthquake, and other non-METOC environmental phenomena where reporting is denied or unavailable.

f. **Special Operations Forces.** Army and Air Force special operations (SO) aviation units can provide PIREPs to support specific missions. Sensors on SOF's manned and unmanned systems can also provide data of meteorological value, including, but not limited to, that from unmanned aerial, maritime, underwater, and ground systems. Limited forward weather observations can be taken by SOF in denied areas and transmitted to the joint SO task force or next echelon weather element on an as required basis. Naval special warfare forces can provide beach profile data as well as surf zone observations. Although these data aid the joint meteorological and oceanographic coordination cell (JMCC) in building a coherent METOC picture, JMOs must be sensitive to OPSEC considerations when incorporating this data into the METOC collection plan. Senior meteorological and oceanographic officers (SMOs) or JMOs should coordinate with the theater SO command METOC branch to identify SOF METOC capabilities specific to the theater of concern.

CHAPTER III
METEOROLOGICAL AND OCEANOGRAPHIC FORCES

> *"The Allies…prevailed because of superior meteorologists…"*
>
> **President Dwight D. Eisenhower on the D-Day Invasion**

1. Introduction

This chapter outlines METOC organizational structure and describes the role of key METOC personnel, units, and forces. The geographic combatant commander (GCC) provides guidance and is responsible for the direction of METOC assets within the area of responsibility (AOR). In some cases, the GCC may designate the SMO to also function as the JMO; the appointment of JMOs should be in line with the combatant command's (CCMD's) METOC concept of operations (CONOPS).

2. Meteorological and Oceanographic Organizations and Staffs

a. **Senior METOC Officer.** Each CCDR may designate a SMO to coordinate all METOC operations within the AOR or functional responsibility. The SMO interacts with the CCDR's staff, the CCMD's components, assigned/attached METOC units, other CCMD SMOs, and other agencies as applicable to ensure unity of effort.

b. **Joint METOC Officer.** The JFC should designate a JMO immediately upon initiation of planning to serve on the JFC staff as the JFC METOC advisor. The JMO plays a critical role in preparing for the success of the joint force mission by supporting all aspects of planning, deployment, and employment. The JMO interacts with the staff components, regional and partner nation (North Atlantic Treaty Organization [NATO]) METOC units, and the SMO to optimize METOC operations.

c. **Meteorological and Oceanographic Operations Support Community (MOSC).** MOSC is an overarching term to describe the units/organizations available to the SMO and/or JMO. As shown in Figure III-1, this could include (but would not be limited to) METOC forecast centers, oceanographic teams, and operational weather squadrons. METOC personnel assigned to a joint task force (JTF) will not normally be sufficient to provide autonomous staff support to the JTF without reachback to the MOSC. The SMO or JMO recommends one unit (a subset of the MOSC) for designation as the joint meteorological and oceanographic coordination organization (JMCO) to support a particular JTF and to coordinate the efforts of all other MOSC units to provide a full suite of products and services to the joint force.

d. **Joint METOC Coordination Organization.** With the advice of the SMO/JMO, the commander, joint task force (CJTF), may request METOC capability from either within the CCMD through a Service component, or outside the CCMD through standard tasking channels. The JMCO is the organization designated by the tasked Service or Service component to provide or arrange for direct support to the JTF. The command relationship between the JTF and the JMCO is that of direct support, with the CJTF being the supported commander and the JMCO commander being the supporting commander.

Refer to Joint Publication (JP) 1, Doctrine for the Armed Forces of the United States, *for detailed roles and responsibilities of supported and supporting commanders.*

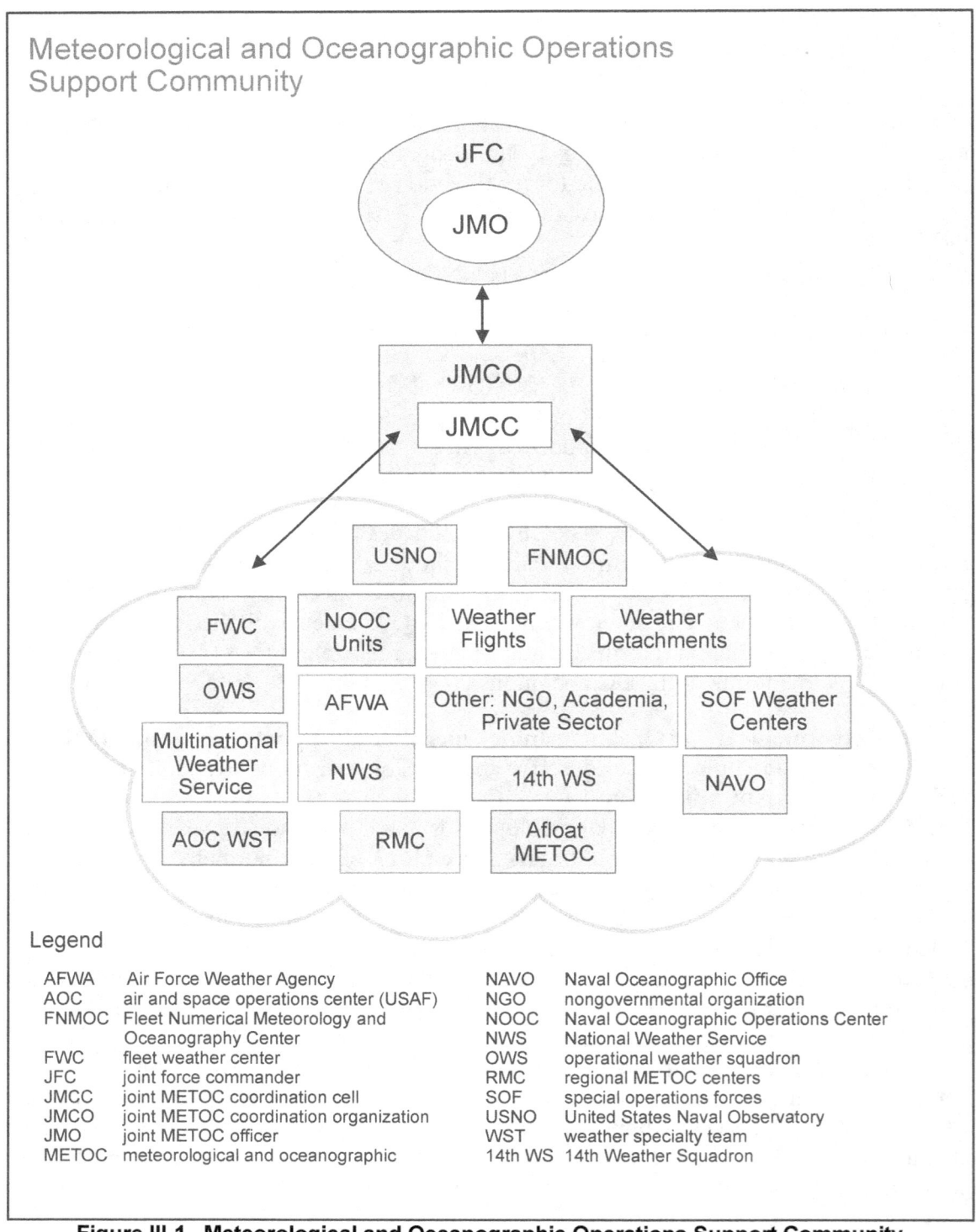

Figure III-1. Meteorological and Oceanographic Operations Support Community

e. The JMCO is normally designated as the lead METOC organization within the OPORD annex H (Meteorological and Oceanographic Operations) and is responsible for coordinating the activities of all MOSC organizations and facilitating METOC operations in support of the JTF. The JMCO should also be listed as a supporting organization to the JFC in annex A (Task Organization) of the OPORD. Selection of an organization from within the MOSC to fill the JMCO role depends on location, capabilities, communications connectivity, and operational considerations. Potential JMCO production facilities and their capabilities are described in the Joint Meteorological and Oceanographic (METOC) Handbook.

f. **Joint METOC Coordination Cell.** The JMCO will normally designate or form a subordinate flight or section, known as the JMCC to provide support to the JTF on a day-to-day basis. Manning of the JMCC will normally be a subset of the hosting METOC unit, with multi-Service augmentation, as required. As the primary tool for achieving unity of effort within the joint operations area (JOA), the JMCC synchronizes and integrates pertinent METOC information in the JOA, leveraging component capabilities and virtually assembling the appropriate MOSC components to meet joint force requirements. The JMCC coordinates support requirements with the SMO/JMO and produces the joint operations area forecast (JOAF) and other METOC products as required by the supported joint force and staffs, on a battle rhythm established by the JMO supporting the JFC's decision cycle. The JMCC and its leadership typically do not deploy to the JOA. The JMCC typically provides support to all joint forces and components in the JOA via reachback. Figure III-2 illustrates the hierarchy of METOC forces in support of a JTF.

3. **Meteorological and Oceanographic Operations: Roles and Responsibilities**

a. **General.** The SMO has a wide range of options in acting as the CCDR's agent for developing and executing a METOC CONOPS, identifying METOC information requirements, and ensuring unity of effort in METOC operations.

(1) The Chairman of the Joint Chiefs of Staff (CJCS), Service, CCDR, subordinate JFC, SMO, and JMO responsibilities for joint METOC operations are provided in CJCSI 3810.01C, *Meteorological and Oceanographic Operations.* SMO and JMO duties and responsibilities are further detailed in this publication.

(2) The duties of the SMO and JMO are similar and complementary during the planning and execution of joint operations. The SMO supports the CCDR in the development and maintenance of established OPLANs and concept plans (CONPLANs), while the JMO supports a JFC in executing a specific mission and/or task by either modifying an existing plan or developing a new one. In all stages of time-phased force and deployment data (TPFDD) development, the SMO and/or JMO need to work with planners to ensure the appropriate mix of Service METOC personnel and equipment are identified for the joint operation. SMO and JMO duties and relationships are discussed below.

Meteorological and Oceanographic Hierarchy in Support of a Joint Task Force

Entity	Scope	Designated by
SMO	CCDR's senior METOC officer	CCDR
JMO	CJTF's senior METOC officer	JFC as advised by the SMO
MOSC	Collection of METOC production and reachback units	
JMCO	MOSC unit with responsibility to coordinate JTF METOC support	OPORD
JMCC	Cell designated to manage/create JTF METOC production Note: May contain METOC forces external to the JMCO when coordinated	Commander of designated JMCO

Legend

CCDR	combatant commander		JTF	joint task force
CJTF	commander, joint task force		METOC	meteorological and oceanographic
JFC	joint force commander		MOSC	METOC operations support community
JMCC	joint METOC coordination cell		OPORD	operation order
JMCO	joint METOC coordination organization		SMO	senior METOC officer
JMO	joint METOC officer			

Figure III-2. **Meteorological and Oceanographic Hierarchy in Support of a Joint Task Force**

b. **SMO Duties.** During the planning and execution of joint operations, the SMO's duties typically include, but are not limited to:

(1) Developing a METOC sensing strategy that leverages Department of State, Department of Commerce, and other United States Government (USG) departments and agencies, as necessary.

(2) Developing an initial METOC collection plan, based on the sensing strategy, during operation and deliberate planning.

(3) Developing and executing a METOC CONOPS that is integrated with, and complements, the CCDR's CONOPS.

(4) Obtaining METOC information requirements from all joint forces, recommending assignment of METOC tasks, and coordinating with components to ensure unity of effort.

(5) Coordinating with the JMO, the Services, and other agencies for METOC support or other additional capabilities required to fulfill operational needs that are not within the components' ability to provide. The SMO does not command the METOC forces in theater and does not specifically task how the Service components perform service-specific or unique tasks. Refer to OPLAN/OPORD annex C (Task Organization).

(6) Ensuring annex H (Meteorological and Oceanographic Operations) is developed for each CCDR's OPORD, OPLAN, or CONPLAN, as appropriate.

(7) Coordinating METOC communication requirements with the CCMD communications system directorate of a joint staff (J-6) and components, and assisting in the development of annex K (Communications Systems Support) of each CCDR's OPORD, OPLAN, or CONPLAN, as appropriate.

(8) Addressing METOC environmental requirements for OPLAN annex N (Space Operations). Coordinating with the US Strategic Command SMO for nonstandard space support requirements.

(9) With the CCDR's approval and the aid of his staff, coordinating with US diplomatic missions, Joint Staff, other USG departments and agencies, and multinational forces, as required, to ensure all available METOC information and systems, as well as indigenous assets and data, are properly considered and made available, if needed, for use by the joint force.

(10) Coordinating requirements with the JFC and the JMO for the establishment, designation, and augmentation of a JMCO. In cases where multiple JFCs are designated and JOAs are contiguous, deconflicting responsibility and operations between the different METOC operations to ensure continuity of the "one operation, one forecast" tenet and potentially assigning a lead JMO for the contiguous JOAs may be considered.

(11) Ensuring all METOC personnel and equipment requirements are included in the TPFDD and that METOC TPFDD requirements are validated.

(12) Collecting after action reports and lessons learned upon completion of joint operations, incorporating lessons learned into revisions of OPLANs and CONPLANs, and providing them to the Services for future programming and planning.

(13) Serving as the focal point for joint force METOC support as outlined in Chapter IV, "Meteorological and Oceanographic Operations in Joint Operation Planning."

(14) Keeping GCC apprised of METOC operations and conditions in the JOA.

For a more comprehensive listing of SMO duties, refer to CJCSI 3810.01C, Meteorological and Oceanographic Operations.

c. **JMO Duties.** During the planning and execution of joint operations, the JMO's duties typically include, but are not limited to:

(1) Integrating METOC impacts into JIPOE, JOPP, commander's situational awareness, C2, and decision making.

(2) Assembling the JFC's METOC staff and equipment.

(3) Advising the JFC on whether to request or establish a JMCO and additional needed METOC capabilities.

(4) Assisting the JFC in developing and executing METOC roles and responsibilities in operational plans and procedures.

(5) Establishing and publishing information requirements and formats, and coordinating METOC operations for the joint force.

(6) Communicating with the SMO and Services for specific METOC capabilities required by deploying forces so they arrive equipped and ready for operational employment. The JMO does not command the METOC forces in theater and does not specifically task how the Service components perform Service-specific or unique tasks.

(7) Monitoring METOC operations within the JOA.

(8) Overseeing JOAF development.

(9) Preparing input to the JFC's situation report to the CCDR.

(10) Requesting additional resources through the JFC.

(11) Coordinating with the SMO and joint staff on updates to the various annexes supporting the OPORD. Specific attention should be given to annexes A, B, C, H, K, M, and N of the OPORD (additional details provided in Appendix C, "Meteorological and Oceanographic Operations Information and Annexes in Operation Plans"), and duties outlined in Chapter IV, "Meteorological and Oceanographic Operations in Joint Operation Planning."

(12) Coordinating with the SMO to ensure all available METOC information and resources, as well as host nation assets, are properly considered and made available for use by joint forces.

(13) Ensuring that all METOC personnel and equipment are included in the TPFDD and coordinating with the SMO to ensure that METOC TPFDD requirements are validated.

(14) Developing, updating, and implementing a METOC collection plan to identify all sources of METOC data across the JOA, using the OPLAN's METOC sensing strategy and initial collection plan as a baseline.

(15) Providing direction to the JMCC supporting the JOA.

(16) Assisting the JFC, the joint staff, and the components to understand the METOC environment in which friendly and enemy weapon systems and/or their supporting infrastructure will operate. The JMO must validate and refine their requirements for METOC information to assist them in planning, conducting, and evaluating operations to achieve the CJTF objectives.

(17) Actively monitoring and evaluating the planning and execution of the operation, and working METOC issues that arise. Providing feedback on the overall performance of the METOC operation effort is critical. The JMO should aggressively work through the JFC's staff for feedback on METOC support. Specify METOC information requirements for inclusion in the CCIRs, priority intelligence requirements, essential elements of friendly information, operational reports, or the OPLAN annex R (Reports).

(18) Evaluating METOC operations at joint-use airfields to provide commanders with recommended COAs for integrating METOC forces into supported operations and avoiding redundancy of deployed METOC capability.

(19) Providing after actions reports and lessons learned to the SMO.

4. Service and Functional Component Meteorological and Oceanographic Forces

a. **General.** Component METOC officers best know the capabilities their forces bring to an operation and how those capabilities can help attain the JFC's objectives and mesh with the METOC forces of the other components. Component METOC officers provide recommendations to their commanders and serve as the focal point for component METOC planning and execution. Based on their component's mission and overall guidance from the SMO or JMO, METOC officers plan, coordinate, and evaluate the METOC support requirements for their component. The METOC officers should document these requirements in appropriate annexes to component level plans. A key duty of METOC officers is to determine which information and products are beyond their capability to provide. In close coordination with subordinate units, each component determines what support it can provide to subordinate units and works with the JMO and JMCO to fill any gaps. Multiple component METOC resources within an operational area will collect METOC data in conjunction with the coordinated METOC collection plan. This data should be integrated to produce METOC products superior to any which an individual component could deliver. Other component duties typically include resolving METOC personnel and equipment problems, identifying shortfalls in METOC personnel and equipment to their staff and SMO or JMO as applicable, and providing input to the TPFDD as required.

b. **Army Forces (ARFOR).** Today's operational focus of the Army emphasizes modular capabilities of the modern BCT. These BCTs attach to a higher echelon headquarters (HQ) (such as a division, corps) as part of a force-tailored formation based on operational requirements. Under this structure, the Army provides land combat power tailored for any combination of offensive, defensive, and stability or civil support operations as part of an interdependent joint force. To provide higher echelon C2, the Army fields a mix of tactical and operational HQ able to function as land force, joint, multinational, and Service component command HQ.

(1) The Air Force provides METOC capabilities to the ARFOR in a direct and general support role as part of the AFFOR (see paragraph 4e, "Air Force Forces (AFFOR)," or Army Regulation [AR] 115-10/Air Force Instruction [AFI] 15-157 Interservice Publication (IP), *Weather Support for the US Army*). To help meet current and emerging Army mission requirements, the Air Force aligns Air Force weather teams with respective Army echelons at the corps, division, brigade, and aviation battalion echelons. The battlefield weather squadrons align personnel and equipment to conduct weather operations, and provide weather services in support of the Army commander's mission. The staff weather officer serves as a member of the Army commanders special or personal staff under the staff supervision of the deputy chief of staff, G-2, or S-2. The mission requirements of each Army echelon will be met using tailored weather teams structured to support joint/Army operations.

(2) **ARTYMET Sections.** ARTYMET sections use a suite of meteorological sensors and large-scale atmospheric data from the AFWA to produce a vertical profile of wind speed and direction, temperature, relative humidity, cloud base height, type precipitation, and horizontal visibility in the target area, all of which are necessary for precise targeting and terminal guidance of various munitions.

(3) In addition, organic Army METOC elements provide two kinds of direct weather support to the Army combat mission. First, ARTYMET sections provide surface and upper-air observations for artillery fire support and nuclear, biological, and chemical downwind prediction. Army personnel use tactical atmospheric sounding and observing equipment to provide this capability. Second, Army military intelligence personnel may provide limited observations from areas where Air Force weather forces are neither manned nor typically operate. These observations can be from manned or automated sensors.

c. **Marine Corps Forces (MARFOR).** Marine Corps METOC is organized as an embedded capability set within selected Marine Corps units (e.g., MACS, intelligence battalions) to support military operations in both garrison and tactical environments. From those units, Marine Corps METOC forces deploy as task-organized teams or detachments with associated expeditionary METOC systems to support the operational requirements of each particular Marine air-ground task force (MAGTF) or mission assignment. Marine Corps METOC capabilities include on-scene sensing/collection, assimilation and processing of raw and processed environmental data, dissemination, and integration of METOC products and services. Marine Corps METOC capabilities facilitate the dynamic characterization and understanding of both the current and future state of the operational environment for MAGTF commanders, planners and warfighters throughout the operational planning process.

d. **Navy Forces (NAVFOR).** Navy METOC personnel provide data collection, assimilation capabilities, products, and services to operating forces ashore and afloat, which are tailored according to the requirements of the component, individual numbered fleet, and task force commanders. Support consists of METOC information for operational use such as tactical decision aids for weapon and sensor system performance and employment, and climatological information for long-range planning.

(1) Navy METOC reachback centers provide on-demand support for naval, joint, multinational, and national missions. The centers act as the point of contact for all forward deployed strike group oceanography teams and mobile environmental teams, operate global and regional METOC models that can be scheduled for on-demand products, provide tailored strategic and tactical sea ice services, and assimilate METOC data worldwide into specific atmospheric and oceanographic models.

(2) Navy fleet survey teams provide high resolution hydrographic surveys for use in nautical or tactical charting and support amphibious landings, mine warfare, or naval special warfare with bathymetry and other collected hydrographic information, enabling access to the littorals.

(3) Navy METOC also provides the positions and motions of celestial bodies, motions of the Earth, and precise time. Astronomical and timing data is required by the Navy and all other components of DOD for navigation, precise positioning, space operations, C2, communications, computers, and intelligence, surveillance, and reconnaissance. The DOD standard for precise time and time interval is Coordinated Universal Time (UTC) as maintained by the USNO. The global positioning system provides most users the means of achieving traceability to UTC (USNO) with an accuracy better than one microsecond. Other methods include atomic clocks, two-way satellite time and frequency transfer, networks, and optical or radio frequency signal transmission.

e. **Air Force Forces (AFFOR).** Air Force METOC forces collect, analyze, and predict METOC data, as well as tailor and integrate METOC information to ongoing operations. Typically, Air Force METOC personnel deployed forward in an AOR perform the collection, tailoring, and integration functions, while most analysis and prediction is performed at the AFWA and subordinate organizations, as well as operational weather squadrons (OWSs). An OWS (or weather flight) normally has the mission to provide direct support to a GCC's AOR up to the Secret level, while AFWA and subordinate organizations provide general support in the form of global forecasting, climatological services, and collection and dissemination of satellite data. In addition, AFWA has the capability to provide direct support to the intelligence community and certain other operators at a higher security classification level. Air Force METOC forces also provide direct and general support to the ARFOR and supported echelons. Air Force METOC forces in support of AFFOR are typically organized as flights under an expeditionary operations support squadron, while those in support of ARFOR are normally organized as flights, detachments, or operating locations under an expeditionary weather squadron. AFFOR retains operational control (OPCON) and administrative control (ADCON) of all Air Force METOC forces deployed in the AOR, including those supporting the Army, though the commander AFFOR may choose to delegate tactical control to the supported Army unit(s).

f. **Special Operations Component.** SOF METOC forces provide METOC operations and tailored services/support to SOF C2 elements, SOF aviation assets, the joint SO air component, and subordinate organizations. Their tailored METOC information and knowledge enable planning, command decisions, and execution of SOF operations. These forces have the capability to plan, coordinate, and conduct METOC operations throughout the operational environment in order to determine METOC impacts to SOF and joint/multinational operations. Air Force SO weather teams and Marine Corps and Navy Oceanography Special Warfare Center METOC forces are trained to operate independently in permissive or uncertain environments, or alongside other SOF elements in hostile environments. SOF METOC reachback centers, such as the 23rd Weather Squadron and the Naval Oceanographic Office Expeditionary and Special Warfare Support Group, provide tailored support to global SOF missions. Implicit capabilities of SOF METOC forces include full integration with other SOF forces in order to conduct atmospheric, oceanographic, and environmental reconnaissance to include terrain reports, METOC training/operations with indigenous personnel, short-term METOC analysis/forecasting, sensor emplacement, weather site surveys for airfields/assault landing zones, and mission tailoring of METOC products. SOF METOC forces are equipped with a variety of Service and SOF equipment to execute these capabilities.

For more information on special operations, refer to JP 3-05, Special Operations.

JOINT TASK FORCE LEBANON

In July 2006, the Secretary of Defense (SecDef) directed a noncombatant evacuation operation (NEO) mission of American citizens from Lebanon, as a result of ground-based hostilites. Elements from US Central Command/Commander, Fifth Fleet (USCENTCOM/COMFIFTHFLT) and US European Command/Commander, Sixth Fleet (USEUCOM/COMSIXTHFLT) surged to the eastern Mediterranean to conduct a sea based NEO.

SecDef established a joint operations area (JOA) and directed Commander, USCENTCOM to execute NEOs as the supported commander. Commander, USCENTCOM tasked the initial mission to COMFIFTHFLT. The COMFIFTHFLT established a forward headquarters at Akrotiri, Cyprus with the IWO JIMA Strike Group and 24th Marine Expeditionary Unit en route from the Gulf of Aqaba. These forces were joined by surface combatants, aviation assets, and other supporting units from USEUCOM. Appointed as the joint METOC officer (JMO), the COMFIFTHFLT oceanographer directed that initial JOA forecasts be developed and issued by organic Navy METOC assets in Bahrain. As the designated joint METOC coordination organization (JMCO), the Bahrain Naval METOC Center also assumed the duties of a joint METOC coordination cell (JMCC) using internal assets and integrated their efforts with the Strike Group Oceanography Team (SGOT) embarked on the USS IWO JIMA.

As the supported commander shifted from Commander, USCENTCOM, to Commander, USEUCOM, JTF LEBANON stood up. Based on USEUCOM SMO recommendation, the JFC designated the COMSIXTHFLT oceanographer to take over JMO duties, and designated the 21st Operational Weather Squadron (OWS) at Sembach, Germany, as the JMCO. The 21 OWS designated a JMCC that generated overland weather support, but received maritime weather and amphibious support from the Naval Maritime Forecast Activity, Norfolk, which also maintained maritime forecasting and ship routing responsibility for all ships in the JOA. The 21 OWS also reached back to the Naval Oceanographic Office for high resolution wave models,

---

surface currents, and other information for the eastern Mediterranean. Upon arrival in the JOA, the SGOT on the USS WASP Strike Group picked up amphibious forecasting responsibilities for the JOA. This variety of METOC support elements coordinated their efforts through twice daily JMCC-led discussions.

Various Sources

Intentionally Blank

CHAPTER IV
METEOROLOGICAL AND OCEANOGRAPHIC OPERATIONS IN JOINT OPERATION PLANNING

> *"In military operations, weather is the first step in planning and the final determining factor in execution of any mission."*
>
> **General Carl Spaatz**
> **Air Force Chief of Staff, 1948**

1. Introduction

a. This chapter complements JP 5-0, *Joint Operation Planning*, to provide assistance to the SMO and JMO involved in planning a joint operation. Early identification of specific support requirements is key to planning.

b. **Planning Requirements.** The size, structure, and content of METOC operations depends on the JFC's operational needs. METOC support includes integrating global, regional, and locally produced METOC products as well as data and products received from supporting agencies and reliable indigenous sources. The SMO incorporates this assessment into a comprehensive sensing strategy and includes it in applicable theater plans. METOC operations should be considered and included in long-range planning, mission planning, and operational execution.

c. **Climatological Data for Planning**. The study and application of historical METOC data/information is invaluable for planning, staging, and executing joint operations and for providing the initial basis for a METOC collection plan. In many cases, especially in developing nations, climatological data or proxy sources (such as local lore or data from other disciplines, e.g., agricultural records) may provide the only METOC data available. Such information includes, but is not limited to, summarized historical METOC information, derived environmental impacts on weapon systems, and tailored narrative studies. Exploiting this information allows the warfighter to take advantage of favorable METOC conditions, minimize impacts of adverse conditions, or use unfavorable METOC conditions to gain advantage.

d. **Installation Survey.** Many sites around the world have been used to collect and disseminate METOC information. Installation surveys provide information on available sensors, communication capabilities, runway criteria, and facilities. These surveys are perishable and need to be periodically updated.

2. Meteorological and Oceanographic Operations in Joint Operation Planning

a. **General.** The Joint Operation Planning and Execution System (JOPES) is the primary system for military operation planning and execution, including requests for forces. Force planning consists of determining the force requirements by operation phase, mission, mission priority, mission sequence, and operating area. SMOs/JMOs ensure appropriate METOC support is provided or requested for joint forces. JFCs, through the SMO or JMO, initiate the requirement for METOC forces to the CCDR. As required, the SMO or JMO should submit a requirement for METOC capabilities, forces, and equipment during planning.

b. **Strategic Guidance.** When an event occurs with possible national security implications and a CCDR's assessment is warranted, the SMO provides valuable input to the CCDR, including:

(1) Current METOC conditions (air, land, maritime, and space) in the AOI.

(2) Climatological factors.

(3) Forecast weather.

(4) Potential METOC impact on the event, to include suitability of sites for employment of forces.

(5) Degree of accuracy and limitations of forecast products.

(6) Potential METOC impact on equipment to include communication, radar, and other sensory equipment.

c. **Concept Development.** During CJCS assessment of the event and review of the CCDR's assessment, METOC supports the determination of whether to initiate military action and provides the possible impacts of METOC conditions on potential military options. It is during concept development that the SMO should develop an initial collection plan for the operation.

d. **Plan Development.** The arrival of a CJCS warning order denotes a critical phase for the SMO. METOC information is integrated into the development of realistic and effective COAs. The SMO and JMO should review the higher HQ order and other appropriate guidance, the commander's initial planning guidance, and with input from subordinate forces determine the specified and implied METOC tasks. The tasking of subordinates to provide input to this process involves another layer of METOC officers who may improve the METOC database for the operating area. A review of the METOC sensing strategy and its application to the JOA should be accomplished to draft a METOC collection plan.

(1) **Collection Planning.** Initial METOC collection requirements are based on analyzing climatological data and the sensing strategy. Climatological analysis identifies specific METOC parameter(s) that when observed or sensed can serve as indicators of future METOC conditions on a grander scale or for specific areas. These weather areas of interest (WAIs) or oceanographic areas of interest (OAIs) are normally aligned with geographic features or arbitrary features such as an engagement area or route. Whenever possible, WAIs/OAIs should be large enough to allow multiple sensing options to collect key METOC data.

(2) The SMO or JMO should next identify critical METOC collection requirements to support the planned operation. The collection plan should identify the WAI and OAI; specify what, when, and why the data is to be collected and lastly, assign a component

METOC force to collect the specified data. It should also leverage sensors on manned and unmanned systems that can provide valuable nontraditional METOC data. This should include autonomous and semiautonomous unmanned undersea and ocean glider systems. The collection plan should identify communication requirements for transmitting, relaying, and/or sharing environmental information so that the collected METOC data can be incorporated into global and regional databases. An operation-tailored and fully coordinated METOC collection plan fosters unity of effort and optimizes METOC data collection.

(3) During plan development, the SMO/JMO identifies and defines METOC requirements in annex H (Meteorological and Oceanographic Operations) and other appropriate annexes of the OPLAN, CONPLAN, OPORD, CONOPS, and/or fragmentary order. Appendix C, "Meteorological and Oceanographic Operations Information and Annexes in Operation Plans," provides guidelines for the preparation of OPLAN annex H (Meteorological and Oceanographic Operations), and details other annexes requiring METOC input. The SMO/JMO should also coordinate the METOC collection plan with the JOA intelligence collection manager for integrating into the operation's overall intelligence, surveillance, and reconnaissance collection plan.

(4) **SMO/JMO Planning Checklist**

(a) **Overview**

1. Have the JMO/JMCO/JMCC designations been promulgated to all participating units, including regional METOC and US support commands?

2. Has the JMO promulgated specific instructions to direct participants?

3. Is there an interagency plan in place?

4. Have efforts been made to pool information with applicable nongovernmental organizations (NGOs) to increase efficiency of operations through coordination and eliminate redundancy in operations?

(b) **Administration**

1. Have METOC billet requirements been identified?

2. Are contact rosters readily available to participants?

(c) **Network**

1. Are limitations in infrastructure and communications considered?

2. Are all units able to connect/work on a common network?

3. Are all METOC units able to collaborate via a common communication tool?

<u>4</u>. Are METOC forces, system capabilities, and support robust enough to respond to increased levels of operational intensity for a long term duration?

(d) **Data**

<u>1</u>. Do all METOC forces have access to the appropriate level of METOC data sources?

<u>2</u>. Has a geospatial information and services (GI&S) plan been produced and disseminated which designates all GI&S products for use?

For a more comprehensive listing of JMO duties, refer to CJCSI 3810.01C, Meteorological and Oceanographic Operations.

For additional information, refer to JP 5-0, Joint Operation Planning, *JP 2-0,* Joint Intelligence, *and JP 2-01.3,* Joint Intelligence Preparation of the Operational Environment.

e. **Plan Assessment.** During this function, the SMO/JMO continuously communicates with the Service component METOC planners to evaluate the situation for any changes that would trigger plan refinement, adaptation, termination, or execution. The goal is to fully support the planned operation.

f. **The Joint Operation Planning Process.** JOPP is a planning model that establishes procedures for analyzing a mission; developing, analyzing, and comparing COAs to criteria of success and to each other; selecting the optimum COA; and producing a plan or order. JOPP applies across the full range of military operations. Commanders and their assigned staffs use JOPP to organize their planning activities, share a common understanding of the mission and commander's intent, and develop effective plans and orders. METOC support is critical to the success of JOPP. Exploiting this information allows the warfighter to take advantage of METOC conditions and minimize impacts of adverse conditions to gain an advantage. The study and application of historical METOC information is invaluable for planning, staging, and executing worldwide military operations. The SMO/JMO must completely understand the assigned mission and provide tailored products during each step of the process to ensure success.

(1) **Initiation.** Upon receipt of the mission, the SMO/JMO reviews the mission of the supported commander and lessons learned from historical operations that may be similar to the assigned mission. They also should review and leverage previously developed plans and orders to include the METOC sensing strategy and initial METOC collection plan.

(2) **Mission Analysis**

(a) The SMO/JMO analyzes the mission assigned to the supported commander and determines the specified and implied METOC tasks. During a contingency, the supported and supporting commander(s) may change depending on the phase of the operation and developing objectives. The SMO/JMO should coordinate closely with the supported components' staff METOC officers on mission impacts and give special consideration to their specific needs as well as identify METOC collection requirements to further develop the METOC collection plan.

(b) **Joint Intelligence Preparation of the Operational Environment (JIPOE).** The SMO/JMO analyzes the military aspects of the METOC environment and then evaluates its direct and indirect effects on military operations. The SMO/JMO provides complete analysis and evaluation as a staff estimate (and updates) to the commander. This estimate will be used to develop COAs to accomplish the mission. A part of JIPOE, geospatial intelligence (GEOINT), is critically important to successful military operations planning, and METOC data is considered an intelligence layer of the GEOINT information base.

For more information on JIPOE, see JP 2-01.3, Joint Intelligence Preparation of the Operational Environment, *and JP 2-03,* Geospatial Intelligence Support to Joint Operations.

(c) Climatology is often used to develop the staff estimate during JIPOE and mission planning. Analyzing the interaction between the air, land, maritime, and space domains is fundamental to successful JIPOE. Due to rapidly changing METOC conditions, the SMO/JMO continuously updates the staff estimate, particularly during mission execution.

(3) **COA Development.** During this step, the SMO/JMO develops valid METOC support COAs. An updated JIPOE provides input to the supported commander's COA development.

The SMO/JMO should develop valid METOC operations support for COAs as described in JP 5-0, Joint Operation Planning.

(4) **COA Analysis and Wargaming.** The SMO/JMO should evaluate partner nation and indigenous capabilities when refining METOC operations support for COAs. At this point, they should refine the METOC support requirements based upon results of the analysis and wargaming. The SMO or JMO should provide an assessment of METOC impacts based on operationally significant METOC sensitivity thresholds impacting the employment of military capabilities being considered in each COA. They should also continue to provide their updated staff estimate to JIPOE.

(5) **COA Comparison.** The SMO/JMO evaluates the METOC operations support requirements for each COA and the ability to meet these requirements. Consideration is given to the pros and cons of each of the METOC support options during this phase. The JMO should ensure that METOC impacts on the employment of military capabilities is included as one of the evaluation criteria during formal COA comparison.

(6) **COA Approval.** The SMO/JMO typically briefs and documents the anticipated impacts of METOC on the commander's COAs. This briefing and documentation serves as the foundation for METOC impacts in the future plan or order. JIPOE is the governing construct for this input. The SMO/JMO should derive relevant assessment measures during this stage and reevaluate them continuously throughout preparation and execution. Generally, the level at which the specific operation, mission task,

or action is directed should be the level at which such activity is assessed. Additionally, the SMO/JMO should coordinate the METOC operations support COA supporting the commander's approved COA. At this stage, the METOC operations support plan should be finalized for inclusion in the OPLAN or OPORD.

(7) **Plan or Order Development.** Plans and orders document METOC operations support to the commander, along with the effects of METOC. The SMO/JMO must be the authoritative source for all METOC inputs to the CCDR and JFC plans, orders, and annexes IAW CJCSI 3810.01C, *Meteorological and Oceanographic Operations.* Coordination with all stakeholders is critical to optimize joint METOC operations and JOPP. Appendix C, "Meteorological and Oceanographic Operations Information and Annexes in Operation Plans," provides additional details on the METOC-related content of OPLAN annexes.

OPERATION EAGLE CLAW: A HARD LESSON TO LEARN

Top-secret planning for what would be one of the most complicated and ambitious raids in American history, the Iranian hostage rescue attempt of 1980, lasted well over five months but it fell short of fully considering an incorrigible foe: the weather.

Historical records pointed to winter as the optimal time for a mission of this type, as limited moonlight and suitable temperatures and densities represented favorable conditions for night RH-53D operations. Nevertheless, the mission was set for late April, introducing additional weather challenges such as suspended dust, which proved to be a factor in the subsequent mishap. This mission-impacting information was never briefed to joint task force (JTF) planners and decision makers...

Recommendations to use a WC-130 weather reconnaissance aircraft as a scout in advance of the RH-53Ds were discounted based on assumed favorable weather conditions and for security reasons. Additionally, it was determined that pilot reports from accompanying C-130s, flying the same route, could provide advance notice of unfavorable weather as needed. However, the C-130s ended up arriving at the destination, Desert One, well ahead of the helicopters and were unable to relay up-to-the-minute weather data to the RH-53D crews.

Weather operations personnel were excluded from planning and rehearsal exercises at the JTF training areas, eliminating their ability to work with the aircrews. Furthermore, mission execution weather briefings, developed by weather operations personnel, were presented by [J-2] joint intelligence officers who had little, if any, formal weather training or experience. Aircrew feedback was provided in the same indirect way. Pilots were thus unaware of the possibility of encountering suspended dust and were unprepared to handle it. Integration of weather information, a vital contributor to mission success, never occurred.

Paul B. Ryan
The Iranian Rescue Mission: Why It Failed

CHAPTER V
EXECUTION OF METEOROLOGICAL AND OCEANOGRAPHIC OPERATIONS

> *"Never in the history of warfare have weather decisions played such an important role in operational planning as they have here in Southeast Asia."*
>
> **General Creighton Abrams**
> **Commanding General, US Military Assistance Command – Vietnam, 1968**

1. General

METOC support normally begins well prior to force deployment and often ends after redeployment of the joint force is complete. Employment planning provides the foundation for, determines the scope of, and is limited by mobilization, deployment, and sustainment planning. METOC forces, databases, products, and equipment must be responsive to the requirements of the JFC and should be maintained to a degree of readiness that ensures immediate employment capability.

2. Deployment

During the deployment process, the movement of capabilities, forces, and equipment occurs in support of the operation IAW the TPFDD. Deployment is primarily the responsibility of the supported commanders and their Service component commanders, in close cooperation with the supporting CCDRs and United States Transportation Command (USTRANSCOM). The four phases of the deployment process are deployment planning; predeployment activities; movement; and joint reception, staging, onward movement, and integration (JRSOI). The SMO/JMO should provide or arrange for METOC operations and support to these phases as outlined:

a. **Deployment Planning.** The SMO/JMO should advise the CCDR/subordinate JFC of any climatological factors that could potentially hamper force deployment. It would be best to identify these factors in annex C (Operations) with specific details in annex H (Meteorological and Oceanographic Operations) of the OPLAN.

b. **Predeployment Activities.** The SMO/JMO should advise the CCDR/JFC of any METOC conditions that could hamper force embarkation, transit, and force debarkation. If identified at this point, the JMCC should be looking across the MOSC for additional information regarding METOC impacts to force deployment.

c. **Movement.** The SMO or JMO should continue to advise the JFC of any METOC conditions that could hamper force embarkation, transit, and force debarkation. The JMCC should continue to monitor the MOSC for additional information, as needed, and prepare to support JRSOI activities.

d. **Joint Reception, Staging, Onward Movement, and Integration Activities.** As JRSOI actions diminish, the SMO/JMO's focus should turn away from force deployment/reception into theater and toward force employment. The JMCC should continue to monitor ports of debarkation and staging areas as warranted when forces transit them, but should now primarily be focused on employment operations.

For additional information, see JP 3-35, Deployment and Redeployment Operations.

3. Employment

a. Communications

(1) The SMO/JMO should consider the communications CONOPS and its ability to support METOC operations as it is a critical component of the plan.

(2) The rapidly changing nature of the air, land, maritime, and space domains makes METOC data extremely perishable. Therefore, effective METOC support to deployed forces in joint operations is dependent upon timely and reliable communications that allow for rapid transfer and refresh rate of METOC data. METOC units share information with each other to facilitate consistency and accuracy of information during an operation. To achieve this level of coordination, all forces involved should have secure communications capability. Communication of METOC information should be designed to fulfill the data collection, storage, retrieval, and dissemination efforts of the METOC forces at all levels. In a broad sense, the concept includes the following:

(a) Information flow among component-level METOC forces within the AOR.

(b) The flow of information between all METOC forces within the AOR. For example, the METOC unit supporting the Army component should be able to access observations, forecasts, and mission impacts from the Navy component. The JMCC is not necessarily the conduit of data flow between existing METOC centers and tactical units, but rather it facilitates data sharing and ensures data is accessible, which may require they act as a conduit at times.

(c) The flow of information from tactical METOC forces back to the component staff METOC officers, the JMCC, the JMO, and throughout and out of the AOR.

(d) The flow of METOC information from outside the AOR into the AOR if reachback is required to other METOC facilities.

(3) Specific responsibilities concerning communications are contained in CJCSI 3810.01C, *Meteorological and Oceanographic Operations.* The following items should be considered to ensure the flow of METOC information throughout the AOR:

(a) Use of a common communications system to the maximum extent possible.

(b) Requirements for satellite broadcast and Global Broadcast System (GBS) support.

(c) Direct access to the Joint Worldwide Intelligence Communications System, SECRET Internet Protocol Router Network (SIPRNET), Nonsecure Internet Protocol Router

Network (NIPRNET), and C2 systems. Multinational operations may require additional network considerations.

(d) Bandwidth considerations for all employed METOC forces must be taken into account. Specific responsibilities concerning communications are contained in CJCSI 3810.01C, *Meteorological and Oceanographic Operations*.

(4) **Early-In and Initial Communications Concept.** Early-in communications equipment must be capable of allowing the METOC forces to support the joint force until sustaining, backbone communications are available. Early-in communications include the GBS, Iridium satellite phones, international maritime satellite terminal, and other Service capabilities.

(5) **Security Considerations.** The JFC is responsible for denial of METOC information to an enemy. Joint METOC forces should use secure communications whenever possible.

b. **JMCC Operations**

(1) The JMCC is the cornerstone of METOC operations support. Typically annex H (Meteorological and Oceanographic Operations), the METOC letter of instruction, and the METOC CONOPS state the JMCC's mission. Under the JMO's direction and guidance, the JMCC synchronizes and integrates all METOC information for the JFC's operational area. Simply stated, the task of the JMCC is to combine multiple source METOC information with operational information to generate the JOAF with a coherent METOC picture. The functionality of the JMCC may differ based on its geographic focus and missions; however, it will typically operate 24 hours per day and should be capable of consolidating the products necessary for the JFC. Once the JMCC is designated by the JMCO, it receives direction and information on planned operations directly from the JMO.

(2) Typical JMCC activities include:

(a) Obtain METOC data.

(b) Analyze METOC data.

(c) Consolidate METOC information from multiple MOSC and indigenous sources. Maximize the use of net-centric capability and operationally-secure web-based technology to build a virtual data warehouse of products. Typically, this can be accomplished through a METOC web page.

(d) Maintain an appropriate level of situational awareness of the joint force operation, the overall objective, and specific METOC thresholds that affect joint force component operations.

(e) Incorporate the JFC's METOC thresholds (restricted and/or unrestricted recommendation and/or decision matrix) that affect military capabilities and joint operations in the field.

(f) Prepare and disseminate the JOAF.

(g) Host JOAF collaborative sessions (e.g., chat sessions, teleconferences).

(h) Prepare and disseminate special support products (e.g., a more detailed forecast including METOC thresholds for a specific operation) as required.

(i) Perform a meteorological watch for the joint force AOI.

(j) Amend and update products as required.

(k) Perform quality control on JOAF and any other products generated by the JMCC.

(l) Conduct assessments of performance and effectiveness.

(m) Provide support to SMO, JMO, joint force METOC components, and joint staff as required.

(n) Prepare report inputs and record lessons learned as required.

(o) Handle classified material, sensitive compartmented information, and/or special access requirements when appropriately cleared.

(3) **Joint Operations Area Forecast**

(a) The JMCC's primary product is the JOAF; it is the official baseline forecast for operational planning and mission execution within the JOA. It provides a discussion of, and rationale for, expected METOC conditions. The JOAF is a dynamic product whose format, content, and duration are determined by operational requirements. The JOAF may have geographic "sub" areas identified within the JOA to further refine the METOC conditions. The JOAF should specify time of occurrence, duration, and intensity when certain METOC parameters are expected to meet or exceed operational thresholds and is amended as required by the JFC. Potential JOAF formats may be any combination of text and graphics as stated by the SMO/JMO. The JMCC must emphasize coordination and consensus among all joint METOC forces to successfully deconflict the JOAF, with the JMO as the final arbiter. Figure V-1 provides examples of METOC parameters addressed in the JOAF.

(b) METOC personnel use the JOAF as a starting point and fuse local data to tailor tactical-level planning and execution products. Component tactical-level forecasts may take a different form based on different mission focus and greater required level of detail. JTF components communicate significant differences between their tactical forecasts and the JOAF with the JMO. Collaboration needs to occur between the JMCC, JMO, and component METOC personnel to maintain a "one operation, one forecast" concept. The JMCC is responsible for making necessary changes to the JOAF and the JMO settles any significant differences between components and/or the JMCC.

Examples of Meteorological and Oceanographic Parameters
Addressed in the Joint Operations Area Forecast

Current and Projected Situation Discussion

This discussion should:

- Address the synoptic and mesoscale meteorological and oceanographic (METOC) situation
- Cover the surface, subsurface, upper-air, and meteorological satellite (METSAT) information
- Highlight significant METOC phenomena in the joint operations area (JOA)
- Provide a summary and assessment of operationally significant METOC phenomena
- Briefly summarize and/or characterize model performance

Forecast

This forecast should detail and/or partition area(s) affected within the JOA as required and forecast, for example, the following criteria:

- Clouds (amounts, bases and/or tops)
- Turbulence (intensity and level[s])
- Icing (type, intensity, and level[s])
- Thunderstorms (intensity and coverage)
- Contrails (levels)
- Predominant wind speed
- Predominant wind direction
- Hail (including size)
- Precipitation (type and intensity)
- Present weather; obstructions to visibility
- Surface visibility
- Surface temperatures (max and/or min)
- Tides
- Littoral currents
- Significant wave height (swell, and/or winds)
- Surf conditions
- Sea surface temperature
- Impacts to the JOA from the space environment
- Surface pressure
- Light data

Figure V-1. Examples of Meteorological and Oceanographic Parameters Addressed in the Joint Operations Area Forecast

c. **METOC Measures of Performance.** METOC measures of performance (MOPs) should continuously be evaluated during execution (see Figure V-2). Monitoring available information and using MOPs, the SMO and JMO determine progress towards achieving operational objectives as well as any required modifications to the METOC CONOPS (e.g., the JMO may determine from assessment and feedback that METOC sensors could be relocated to achieve better overall collection effectiveness). Modifications to the METOC CONOPS will form the basis of, and serve as a source for, lessons learned and after action reports.

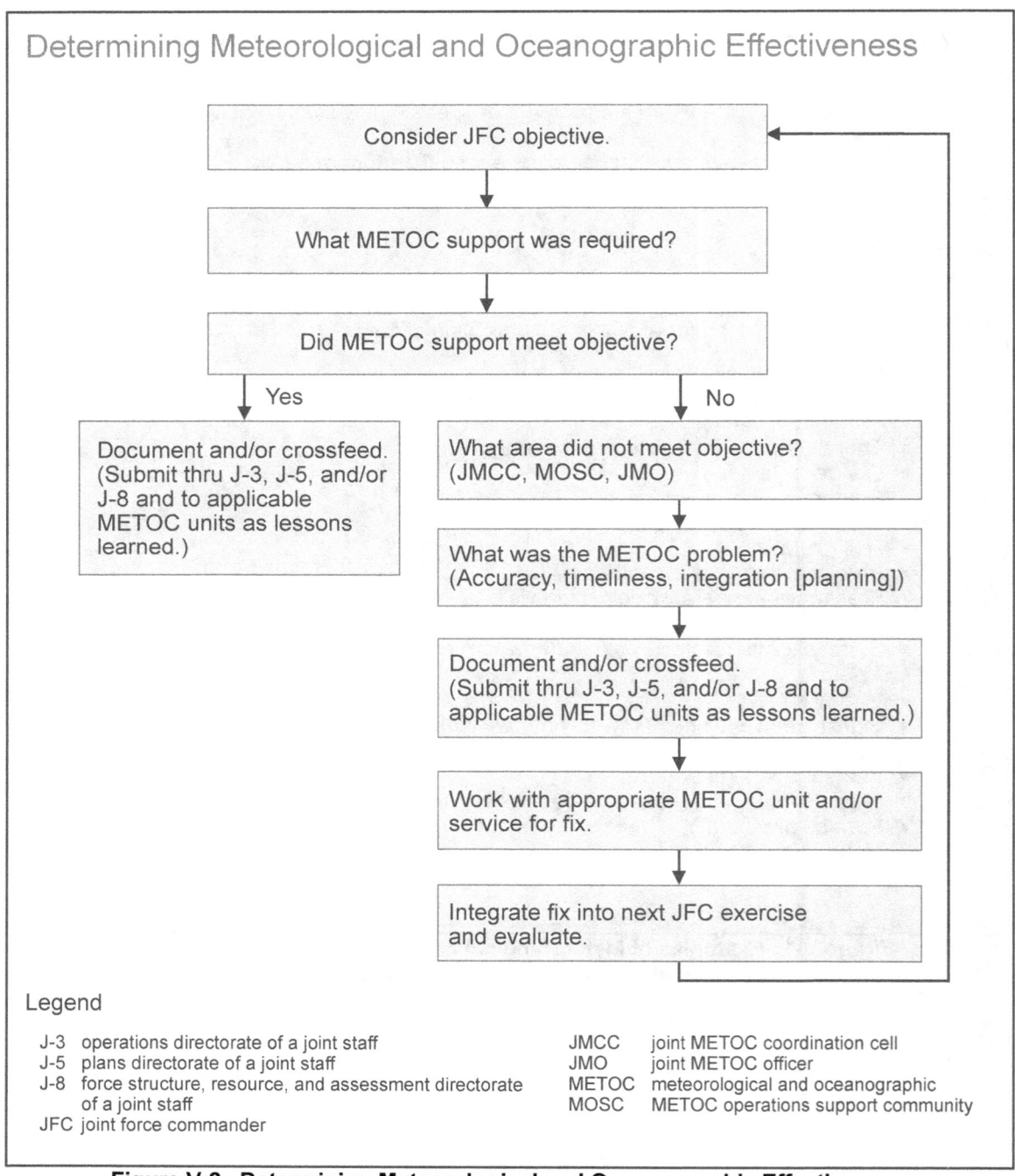

Figure V-2. Determining Meteorological and Oceanographic Effectiveness

For more information on assessment of operational effectiveness, refer to JP 5-0, Joint Operation Planning.

d. **METOC Support to Foreign Humanitarian Assistance Operations and Defense Support of Civil Authorities Operations**

(1) **Support to Foreign Humanitarian Assistance Operations.** A humanitarian crisis could result from wartime, other military action, or a natural/man-made disaster. These operations may require SMO/JMO interaction and coordination with other nations' civil or military METOC personnel. Circumstances will dictate the amount of METOC support required.

(2) Defense support of civil authorities (DSCA) operations are typically initiated in response to a natural disaster or other domestic emergency and require interaction and coordination with other federal agencies. National Guard forces may respond to humanitarian or civic assistance missions in the continental US. When National Guard forces become involved, the SMO/JMO recommends establishment of the appropriate relationships (ADCON, OPCON, or tactical control) of the additional forces. However, it is recommended that METOC support to DSCA missions mirror deployed operations when appropriate. For additional details regarding DSCA, refer to Appendix B, "Defense Support of Civil Authorities and Interagency Operations within the United States."

For more information on DSCA and foreign humanitarian assistance, refer to JP 3-28, Defense Support of Civil Authorities, *and JP 3-29,* Foreign Humanitarian Assistance.

e. The SMO/JMO should be prepared to engage in some level of nation assistance as part of stability operations conducted concurrently with combat operations or post-conflict operations. The level of effort will depend on the CCDR/subordinate JFC direction, and these tasks will generally fall under the umbrella of a larger military assistance training team. Items the SMO/JMO should bear in mind while gearing up this effort include: joint manning document positions, an overall CONOPS, training topics/objectives, and an overall implementation plan.

4. Redeployment

Redeployment operations are conducted to reposture forces and materiel in the same theater, to transfer forces to support another JFC, or return personnel and materiel to home station or demobilization location. The SMO/JMO's and JMCC's attention should once again be on port operations. The SMO/JMO should advise the GCC/JFC of environmental features which would hamper the redeployment process.

**OPERATION UNIFIED ASSISTANCE:
DECEMBER 2004**

The Navy's Fleet Survey Team (FST) is designed to conduct quick response hydrographic surveys and produce charting products in the field for maritime requirements. C-130 deployable elements of the FST can conduct navigation quality surveys or clearance surveys to provide access to ports and waterways in support of operations from amphibious landings to humanitarian assistance and disaster relief. Detachments can utilize FST's organic rigid hull inflatable boats, US Navy small boats, or host country vessels of opportunity to install and operate precision hydrographic gear.

Following the Boxing Day Tsunami in Indonesia, survey teams were immediately on-scene to conduct safety of navigation surveys in support of humanitarian aid/disaster relief operations along the northwestern coast of Sumatra, Indonesia. Four harbors (Meulaboh, Bande Ache, Lamno, and Lho Kruet) were surveyed in order to ensure harbors and approaches were free of debris. The surveys were conducted using two seven-meter RHIBs launched from USS Benfold (DDG 65). The eight-person team completed four check surveys and produced four field charts in less than three weeks. Efforts by the team not only provided critical information to Combined Support Force 536 and inbound relief vessels, but also opened doors for future cooperation between the US and Indonesian governments.

The FST meets international standards for hydrographic surveying and works closely with the National Geospatial-Intelligence Agency, the National Oceanic and Atmospheric Administration, and the US Army Corps of Engineers.

Various Sources

For additional information, see JP 3-35, Deployment and Redeployment Operations.

APPENDIX A
SUPPORT REQUIREMENTS AND RESPONSIBILITIES IN MULTINATIONAL OPERATIONS

1. Multinational Operations

Multinational operations is a collective term to describe military actions conducted by forces of two or more nations. In multinational operations, early planning is critical. Differences in language, techniques, data formats, and communications should be overcome prior to any operation. The multinational force commander (MNFC) should designate a lead multinational METOC officer to coordinate METOC support and interoperability. This officer monitors, synchronizes, and when appropriate, integrates all METOC operations to ensure "one operation, one forecast" and that all METOC requirements are met. For situations where a multinational force is operating in parallel with another coalition (e.g., NATO), only one may be designated the SMO.

For a more detailed explanation of multinational operations refer to JP 3-16, Multinational Operations, *and JP 5-0,* Joint Operation Planning.

2. Multinational Considerations

a. **Planning Considerations in Multinational Operations.** Planning for multinational operations is accomplished in multinational and national channels. MNFCs develop multinational strategies and plans in multinational channels. JFCs perform supporting joint operation planning for multinational operations in US national channels. Coordination of these separate planning channels occurs at the national level by established multinational bodies or coalition member nations and at the theater-strategic and operational levels by JFCs, who are responsible within both channels for operation planning matters.

b. **Planning Checklist.** Detailed planning checklists for multinational operations can be found in JP 3-16, *Multinational Operations.*

(1) Has the OPLAN annex H (Meteorological and Oceanographic Operations) been coordinated with national and interagency partners?

(2) Have appropriate METOC inputs been incorporated into other OPLAN annexes and coordinated with national and interagency partners?

(3) Have command relationships been established between the MNFC and national METOC forces?

(4) Have METOC billet requirements been identified?

(5) Have the personnel for the multinational METOC staff been chosen to reflect the required functional skills, training level, and language skill requirements.

(6) Are there sufficient interpreters available for both planning and execution?

(7) Do liaison elements have appropriate linguistic, communications, logistic, and office support capabilities in place?

(8) Have the multinational partners with a lesser C2 capability been provided appropriate liaison personnel and interpreters (if necessary), operators, and maintainers to enable interaction with the commander and other multinational members?

(9) Have arrangements been made for intra- and inter-staff communication among same-nation staff members?

(10) Have efforts been made to pool information with applicable NGOs to increase efficiency of operations through coordination and eliminate redundancy in operations?

(11) Are forces, METOC system capabilities, and support robust enough to respond to increased levels of operational intensity?

(12) Has coordination been accomplished with multinational members regarding METOC equipment capability?

(13) Do all multinational METOC forces have access to the appropriate level of METOC data sources (e.g., World Meteorological Organization sources, joint Air Force and Army weather information network, indigenous or host nation sources)?

(14) Have agreements on cryptographic, communications and/or automated data processing (ADP) security issues, and other planning factors been reached among all multinational components? Are compatible materials available (where appropriate)?

(15) Have arrangements been made or established to allow contract multinational foreign nation employees to work on METOC staffs without exposure to ADP and classified information used in daily operations?

(16) Have the nations agreed to work on a standard map datum (e.g., World Geodetic System 1984) and produce all products to that datum?

(17) Has a multinational GI&S plan been produced and disseminated which designates all GI&S products for use?

(18) Have special, adequate, and supportable METOC data sharing and foreign disclosure procedures been established?

(19) Have efforts been made to assign METOC data gathering tasks IAW the MNFC's METOC requirements and according to the capability of the multinational equipment under multinational control?

(20) Have efforts been made to pool METOC and battlefield weather information into multinational centralized processing centers?

c. **Operational Considerations**

(1) **Data Collection.** Multinational operations depend on the timely collection and sharing of high quality METOC data. The foundation for effective METOC operations is set by observations from air, land, maritime, and space by personnel, sensors, or platforms.

(2) **METOC Collection Plan.** A comprehensive collection plan ensures unity of effort while optimizing data collection, dissemination, and integration into METOC databases, models, and forecast products. Spreading observation resources across an AOI with regard to climatic zones to obtain optimal coverage will significantly improve the quality of METOC services. The commander's objectives will drive the collection plan in some cases.

(3) **Forecasting.** The JMCC and other forecast elements develop specific METOC products to enhance multinational operations and to meet joint requirements. METOC forecasts can be developed for the near or far term to cover strategic, operational, and tactical scales.

(4) **METOC Centers.** Depending on the operation and level of support required, the JMCC or other designated reachback and production centers will ensure METOC operations support a "one operation, one forecast" concept. A unified weather forecast is the primary mechanism to ensure METOC consistency across an operation. The primary tool used to accomplish this concept is the JOAF; its use in planning multinational operations will ensure commanders at all levels are planning from the same anticipated METOC conditions. In multinational operations, where the US may not have lead forecast unit responsibility, special consideration and effort are required to maintain "one operation, one forecast."

For more detailed explanation of NATO METOC operations, refer to NATO MCM-0178-2005, Integrated METOC Support Concept (IMETOC), *24 October 2005.*

OPERATION TOMODACHI
11 MARCH – 04 MAY 2011

On March 11, 2011, a magnitude 9.0 earthquake struck northern Japan, causing widespread damage and triggering a massive tsunami. A US Joint Support Force (JSF) was organized to direct humanitarian assistance and disaster relief (HA/DR) while also monitoring a potential radiation hazard at a failing Japanese nuclear power plant.

The joint meteorological and oceanographic (METOC) structure was originally established to facilitate an HA/DR operation, but was immediately challenged by a broad interagency problem involving US Navy, US Air Force, National Oceanic and Atmospheric Administration (NOAA), Defense Threat Reduction Agency (DTRA) and Japanese defense force and civil authorities. Although challenged by geographic distance and limited communications, the senior METOC officer and joint METOC officer worked closely together to take advantage of combatant command interagency resources, component expertise and United States support offices (NOAA and the Naval Oceanographic Office) to achieve coordination between the various agencies and organizations participating in the operation. As the scope of the nuclear disaster came into focus, the JSF commander's highest priority information requests involved critical environmental factors that were driving the circulation of air and ocean borne radiation. Through close and detailed coordination with DTRA and data support from Japanese agencies, US Navy and US Air Force METOC, and NOAA, the JSF commander was supported with an accurate depiction of the operational environment for planning and execution.

The vital support of the JSF by the Joint METOC structure enabled an efficient relief effort while providing critical information to ensure the safety of the force.

Various Sources

APPENDIX B
DEFENSE SUPPORT OF CIVIL AUTHORITIES AND INTERAGENCY OPERATIONS WITHIN THE UNITED STATES

1. Defense Support of Civil Authorities

a. DSCA primarily requires operational DOD interagency coordination to plan, prepare, and execute its mission.

b. DSCA is initiated by a request for DOD assistance from civil authorities or qualifying entities or is authorized by the President or Secretary of Defense. DOD METOC capabilities employed in support of DSCA operations should be deconflicted and synchronized with national level METOC capabilities.

For additional information on DSCA, refer to JP 3-28, Defense Support of Civil Authorities, *and DODD 3025.18,* Defense Support of Civil Authorities.

2. Meteorological and Oceanographic Concept of Operations for Interagency Requirements

a. General US interagency coordination within the METOC community is conducted by the Office of the Federal Coordinator for Meteorological Services and Supporting Research. However, for specific time-sensitive DOD support to other US agencies, the CCMD, as the supported commander, may take the lead for interagency coordination; within the METOC community, the CCMD SMO normally becomes the DOD focal point for METOC coordination between non-DOD agencies and supporting military forces.

b. The CCMD SMO and designated subordinate JMOs are responsible for ensuring METOC support to CJTFs and assigned forces is consistent with METOC information provided to the organizations and agencies supported by those forces. While support to DOD forces is normally provided by their traditional Air Force and Navy METOC providers, the SMO/JMO may direct the Service METOC providers to ensure their products are consistent with those produced by the National Weather Service (NWS) or official local or state meteorologists (to include state National Guard METOC), especially for locations where DOD and civil responders are working in the same areas. For most locations throughout the US, the NWS is the authoritative source for official forecast and related information. Additionally, the US Air Force, Air National Guard (ANG), and US Navy originate aviation and area forecasts for airfields and bases under their cognizance. The NWS has established a homeland securities activities lead at the Department of Homeland Security (DHS) to serve as the primary liaison for the SMOs with the NWS. During a USG response, the NWS will normally name a particular weather service field office to serve as the lead METOC organization; much like the JMCO is the lead for the DOD response. The SMO/JMO typically coordinates with NWS to establish collaborative processes, such as conference calls among lead NWS offices and appropriate US military METOC offices. When DOD forces support civil agencies, the SMO/JMO will normally provide copies of a DOD METOC letter of instruction or CONOPS to supporting NWS offices and ANG

METOC personnel, as well as all participating Title 10, United States Code (USC) METOC personnel and appropriate military strategic and regional centers.

c. For METOC coordination with the US Coast Guard, the SMO works through the CCDR's staff Coast Guard liaison officer to determine which organization (US Naval organization, NWS, or a Federal Aviation Agency office) is providing METOC support for missions of interest, and works with that office and the Coast Guard to ensure forecasts remain consistent regardless of source.

d. The SMO/JMO is also responsible to plan and manage the disposition and employment of METOC personnel and equipment supporting military forces or airfields within the US normally through command OPORDs or fragmentary orders, and by submitting requests for forces as required. During employment, ANG METOC personnel operating under Title 32, USC, remain under the authority of their state governor. However, mobilization in federal active duty status and deployment of ANG METOC forces in support of the CCMD may be necessary to provide direct support to joint operations.

e. The SMO also works with NWS to maintain awareness of the current state of DHS efforts to provide a single, authoritative forecast of METOC information in support of the offices that produce depictions of hazardous clouds or plumes. In case of a weapon of mass destruction incident, the METOC and CBRN support personnel within the CCMD staff, in conjunction with the Defense Threat Reduction Agency (DTRA), must ensure the CCDR and forces are provided the same accurate, authoritative forecast as that provided by US civil counterparts. The Interagency Modeling and Atmospheric Assessment Center (IMAAC) as the single federal source of airborne hazard predictions for DHS once a CBRN incident is declared a National Security Special Event. The federal partners for the IMAAC include DHS, DOD, Department of Energy, Environmental Protection Agency, National Oceanic and Atmospheric Administration (NOAA) (Department of Commerce), Nuclear Regulatory Commission, Department of Health and Human Services, and National Aeronautics and Space Administration. The IMAAC collects the appropriate agencies' modeling efforts and coordinates with the modeling centers of the federal agency partners listed above. This coordination ensures standardization of modeling source terms, material type and amount, location and time, expulsion parameters, and meteorology. Each federal agency partner is expected to present their modeling assumptions, and the meteorological parameters. The IMAAC then evaluates the various plumes for methodology of modeling, verification of known parameters, and consistency of output. The federal agency partners are to then nominate a single realization of the CBRN plume output. This result is then fed back to all the partners for refinement of their models, and forwarded to key leadership for situational awareness. The core concept behind the IMAAC is that a single, coordinated "plume model output" is sent to all necessary DHS decision makers to include the on-scene commander through national leadership. CCMD METOC personnel should coordinate with DTRA to receive the latest information on the meteorological data used in the creation of the subject plume. Some agencies will utilize METOC data not readily available to the CCMD personnel. In that case, DTRA will attempt to gain access to that data or provide a suitable substitute, deconflicting and ensuring consistency in METOC parameters are maintained to the greatest extent possible.

f. The SMO maintains relationships with other Federal and international agencies, such as the National Interagency Fire Center, the NOAA/Space Weather Prediction Center, the Canadian Department of National Defence, Environment Canada, NOAA, Joint Typhoon Warning Center, Navy and Air Force METOC organizations and activities, US Geological Service, and other DOD organizations to ensure consistent forecasts in support of DSCA in order to maintain a "one operation, one forecast" construct within the US.

Intentionally Blank

APPENDIX C
METEOROLOGICAL AND OCEANOGRAPHIC OPERATIONS INFORMATION AND ANNEXES IN OPERATION PLANS

SECTION A. INTRODUCTION

1. **Overview**

This appendix describes METOC information necessary for inclusion in OPLANs. It also summarizes standard locations where METOC information is used within the JOPES. The information in this appendix is provided to aid the SMO/JMO in determining where and what type of METOC information can be integrated with other staff functions as the JFC's plan develops. JMOs should work with the appropriate joint staff directorates to ensure METOC guidance and information provided in other functional annexes are complete and accurate. The JMO is responsible for METOC information commonly used in the intelligence estimate, the commander's estimate of situation, and OPLAN annexes A, B, C, D, H, K, M, N, P, R, and V. The SMO is responsible for METOC information commonly used by CCMD staffs, which may serve as a basis for OPLANs. The information in this appendix for OPLANs may be used as a guide for the contents of standard plan annexes. The SMO will determine the appropriate contents of these annexes as they apply to the AOR versus a JOA.

For more information, refer to Chairman of the Joint Chiefs of Staff Manual (CJCSM) 3122.03C, Joint Operation Planning and Execution System (JOPES) Volume II, Planning Formats.

SECTION B. METEOROLOGICAL AND OCEANOGRAPHIC INFORMATION IN MAIN OPERATION PLAN

2. **Intelligence Estimate**

a. Accurate and timely METOC information can help in the formulation of an accurate intelligence assessment. Reconnaissance assesses the topography, terrain, and approaches and exits from borders; natural obstacles; the nature of the coastline; adjacent islands; location, extent, and capacity of landing beaches and their approaches and exits; and the nature of the offshore approaches, including type of bottom and gradients; natural obstacles; and surf, tide, and ocean and/or water current conditions.

b. The intelligence estimate requires METOC parameters such as temperature, humidity, cloud cover, visibility, precipitation, illumination data, and other METOC conditions to assess effects on roads, airfields, rivers, and soil trafficability, including tactical impacts on both friendly force and enemy capabilities. From these METOC specifications, GEOINT analysts can assist in accurately determining the METOC effects on GEOINT sensing capabilities, enemy capabilities and possible COAs for friendly and enemy forces.

3. Commander's Estimate of the Situation

The commander's estimate will include the characteristics of currents, tides, and similar maritime considerations, and determine and state extremes of temperature, wind velocities, cloud cover, visibility, precipitation, and other such factors that can affect all military operations. Sunrise and sunset, moonrise and moonset, civil, nautical, and/or astronomical twilight data, and moon percent illumination are also normally provided.

SECTION C. METEOROLOGICAL AND OCEANOGRAPHIC INFORMATION IN OPERATION PLAN ANNEXES

4. Annex A, Organization

Annex A should list the MOSC elements and JMCC functions which will be used by the METOC forces in the AOR. JMOs should refine the annex A for the specific JTF mission.

5. Annex B, Intelligence

Annex B should summarize the hydrographic data (water depths, tides, wave height, and currents) needed to support amphibious, logistics over-the-shore, and expeditionary operations. Reference annex H and any others (C, K, N, etc.) as required; include climatology and weather aspects as they pertain to the operational environment; and perform a thorough intelligence preparation of the operational environment from a METOC perspective. Specific elements of annex B can be found in CJCSM 3122.03C, *Joint Operation Planning and Execution System (JOPES) Volume II, Planning Formats*.

6. Annex C, Operations

Annex C should summarize METOC operations and forces documented in annex H. Annex C details on joint force operations are critical to completing the METOC input for annexes B, M, and H. Annex C will summarize the general nature of METOC phenomena or conditions, with emphasis on those that could have an impact on the main and supporting efforts of the operation, as well as any planned deception actions.

7. Annex D, Logistics

Annex D should document special logistic support required by the METOC forces, as required.

8. Annex H, Meteorological and Oceanographic Operations

Annex H describes METOC operations and services within a joint force. It is the SMO/JMO's primary vehicle to provide directive guidance on tasks and responsibilities, coordinating instructions, and the joint METOC CONOPS. Additionally, strategic and operational-level and tactical-level METOC MOPs should be identified in this annex.

a. List documents that provide information required for use with this annex.

b. State the general concept of METOC operations and the forces apportioned to the supported CCDR to execute the OPLAN. State the assumptions that affect the METOC operations required by the plan to include availability of facilities and support from non-US and US nonmilitary agencies.

c. Identify and define the METOC sensing strategy or data collection plan requirements as appropriate for the operation. Include realistic estimates of the availability of data from DOD METOC and non-DOD METOC sources and the feasibility of obtaining METOC data from nontraditional satellites and unmanned systems.

d. Identify any significant METOC conditions that may influence the execution of the plan. The purpose of this paragraph should be to establish the requirement for any unusual METOC operations that will clarify the assignment of specific responsibilities. METOC factors that may influence operations and the probability of their occurrence will be included.

e. State clear and concise METOC operational objectives in support of the plan.

f. Describe the METOC support system and how it will function in the implementation of the plan. Refer to other documents available to tasked units that establish doctrine and procedures, as appropriate. Note any deviations from standard practices and any additional procedures peculiar to the operation.

g. Identify the Service component(s) responsible for providing METOC support to the operation, including communications and production responsibilities for METOC information. Assign responsibilities to specific Service components. Ensure OPSEC planning guidance is included so as to not reveal indicators of friendly intentions. Clearly delineate, for each applicable component or other subdivision of the force, individual METOC services, tasks, and responsibilities. Ensure severe weather notification procedures are outlined for each METOC agency throughout the AOR.

h. **Coordinating Instructions.** Include the instructions common to two or more components or subdivisions.

i. **Administration and Logistics.** Provide broad guidance on how logistic and administrative support is to be furnished for the METOC forces (a reference to the OPLAN's annex D or other pertinent command directives may suffice).

j. **Command and Control.** Indicate the channels for control of METOC operations, if different from the command relationships outlined in the basic plan or in annex J. Provide instructions to cover periods when communication circuits are not operational. Provide instructions for transmitting METOC information to units where METOC or standard C2 circuits are not available. Provide instructions for denying METOC data and information to the enemy through implementation of control of meteorological information, oceanographic information, ice information, and space information. Provide a short description of strategic and tactical communications architectures that will be developed to support METOC data transmission and information flow. Current information condition level should be considered when preparing to conduct collaborative sessions.

9. Annex K, Communications Systems Support

Communications is an essential element of METOC operations. Because METOC data is extremely perishable, effective METOC operations are dependent on timely, reliable communications support. Special attention must be given to including METOC in the communication architecture. The joint communications architecture should support the collection or interception, storage and retrieval, dissemination, quality control, and processing of large amounts of data. High-speed communications are required to rapidly transmit and receive real-time global scale METOC information between the MOSC(s), JMCO, JMCC, component, and tactical units. However, solar activities can impair communication capabilities and should be planned for accordingly. The SMO/JMO should work with the J-6 to determine the overarching backbone communication architecture needed for weather operations. METOC communications concept, procedures, and requirements to support METOC information flow throughout the JOA, to include outage backup procedures, should be included in this annex. They should also coordinate with J-6 on the development of the technical details in annex K (e.g., network diagrams that identify all connections). In general, the METOC providers are subscribers to the Defense Information Systems Network and to the tactical communication resources listed in annex K. Annexes H and K will not list all of the communications resources used.

10. Annex M, Geospatial Information and Services

National Geospatial-Intelligence Agency (NGA) provides a broad range of data in support of DOD METOC requirements. For safety of navigation, NGA uses bathymetric, hydrographic, gravimetric, aeronautical, and topographic information to produce, maintain, and participate in the distribution of maps, charts (nautical and aeronautical), and related materials to support military operations and safety of ship, aircraft, and land navigation. This data includes global foundation data, as well as multiple analytic products and data used to identify, characterize, and target entities of interest to the CCDR. As an intelligence and combat support agency, NGA provides both the standard data listed below and additional data that includes analysis derived from various imagery and imagery-related sensors. Expertise and analysis capabilities resident at the national level are available to the CCDRs and Services via a reachback process. The SMO/JMO should ensure that any METOC requirements for GI&S are included in this annex. This should include any special METOC products formatted geospatially, METOC input to geospatial databases, and any special oceanographic/hydrographic survey requirements, such as a rapid environmental assessment. The list below summarizes primary products produced by NGA in support of METOC that may be requested or addressed in annex M.

For more information, refer to JP 2-03, Geospatial Intelligence Support to Joint Operations.

a. **Nautical/Hydrographic Products**

(1) **Hydrographic Charts.** Coastal; approach; and harbor charts.

(2) **Digital Nautical Charts (DNCs).** The DNCs provide worldwide databases of nautical information in vector product format. These databases will be contained on 29

compact discs read-only memory (CD-ROMs) with each CD-ROM covering a specific geographic area of the world. The data content and coverage are intended to closely replicate NGA's harbor, approach, coastal, and general chart series. The DNCs consist of data partitioned into harbor, approach, coastal, and general libraries, based upon the scale of the source chart.

(3) **Digital Bathymetric Database Variable (DBDB-V).** The DBDB-V format provides ocean depths at various gridded resolutions to support the generation of bathymetric chart products, and to provide bathymetric data to be integrated with other geophysical and environmental parameters for ocean modeling. Depths are given in not tidally corrected meters for each five minutes of latitude and longitude worldwide. A classified version is also available covering the northern hemisphere at a higher data density.

(4) **Fleet Guides.** These provide port information unique to the Navy that is not available elsewhere. Port commands contribute to the overall effectiveness by providing information related to the facilities and services available. Fleet Guides consist of two volumes (Atlantic and Pacific).

(5) **Maritime Safety Information.** Additional maritime safety information and products like bathymetric navigation planning charts, nautical chart symbols and abbreviations, and publications for mariners can be found on the website at http://pollux.nss.nga.mil/.

(6) **Notice to Mariners (NTM).** Contains corrections to unclassified hardcopy hydrographic products produced by NGA, NOAA's National Ocean Service, and the US Coast Guard.

(7) **Force Protection Port Graphics.** The primary assessment tool for USTRANSCOM to determine required antiterrorism/force protection measures. An image-based product with a vector overlay of the following force protection information: seawalls, floodlights, spotlights, large light standards near/on docks, entry control points/guard shacks, hard surface major roads, both single- and multilane, fence lines, and railroads.

(8) **Sailing Directions.** Provide the informational arm to the DNC and/or standard nautical chart. Each publication gives the mariner a unique perspective by bringing to life the information graphically represented by the chart. The worldwide portfolio consists of 37 enroutes (coastal) and 5 planning guides (ocean basin).

(9) **Tactical Ocean Data (TOD).** TOD provides worldwide databases of nautical information in Vector Product Format, in Levels 0, 1, 2, and 4.

(a) TOD Level 0 (TOD0) data content and coverage is intended to closely replicate NGA's Naval Operating Area Chart, Range Chart, and Naval Exercise Area Chart series. TOD0 must be used in conjunction with the DNC to provide feature coverage necessary for surface navigation. The NGA NTM supports the product with maintenance information also on the NGA Maritime Safety Information Center web site.

(b) The TOD Level 1 (TOD1) content and coverage is intended to closely replicate NGA's Bottom Contour Chart series. TOD1 must be used in conjunction with the DNC to provide feature coverage necessary for subsurface navigation. The NGA classified notice to mariners (CNM) supports TOD2 with maintenance information. To be added to the distribution for CNM, send a request to HQ NGA, ATTN: PVM.

(c) The TOD Level 2 (TOD2) data content and coverage is intended to closely replicate NGA's Bathymetric Navigation Planning Chart series. TOD2 must be used in conjunction with the DNC to provide feature coverage necessary for subsurface navigation. The NGA CNM supports TOD2 with maintenance information. To be added to the distribution for CNM, send a request to HQ NGA, ATTN: PVM.

(d) The TOD Level 4 (TOD4) is a vector-based digital product that portrays detailed bathymetric data for submarine hull integrity test sites in a format suitable for computerized subsurface navigation. TOD4 data is designed for use during submarine hull integrity tests conducted as a part of builder's trials and after submarine hull maintenance. TOD4 data is provided primarily to support deep submergence rescue vessel operations and to enhance coordination between units during escorted test dives. TOD4 is intended to be used in conjunction with the DNC and TOD2 to provide feature coverage necessary for surface and subsurface navigation. The NGA NTM supports the product with information on the NGA Maritime Safety Information Center web sites. The NGA CNM supports TOD4 with maintenance information. The TOD4 also functions as a general purpose database designed to support geographic information system applications.

(10) **World Vector Shoreline - Plus.** A digital data file containing the shorelines, international boundaries, and country names of the world. These geographic features are required for many of the digital databases being used to support geographic information systems and weapons systems.

b. **Topographical/Terrestrial Products**

(1) **Topographic Line Map.** Portrays the greatest detail of topographic and cultural information in a standard view. The map is a true representation of terrain detail with relief shown by contours and spot elevations.

(2) **Digital Terrain Elevation Data (DTED).** A uniform matrix of terrain elevation values which provides basic quantitative data for all military systems that require terrain elevation, slope, and/or surface roughness information.

(3) **Controlled Image Base (CIB).** An unclassified seamless dataset of orthophotos, made from rectified, grayscale aerial images. CIB supports various weapons, theater battle management, mission planning, digital moving map, terrain analysis, simulation, and intelligence systems. CIB data are produced from digital source images and are compressed and reformatted to conform to the raster product format standard. CIB files are physically formatted within a National Imagery Transmission Format message. CIB may be derived from a grayscale image, from one band of a multispectral product, or from an arithmetic combination of several multispectral bands. Applications for CIB include rapid

overview of areas of operations, map substitutes for emergencies and crises, metric foundation for anchoring other data in communications systems or image exploitation, positionally-correct images for draping in terrain visualization, and image backgrounds for mission planning and rehearsal.

(4) **Vector Map (VMap).** Designed to provide vector-based geospatial data at various resolutions, generally from cartographic sources. Data is separated into ten thematic layers consistent throughout the VMap program.

(5) **Shuttle Radar Topography Mission DTED.** Describes the radar reflective surface of landmasses down to 30-meter post spacing. DTED is useful in intervisibility computations and three-dimensional fly-throughs.

(6) **City Graphic.** A large-scale map of populated places and environs portraying streets and through-route information. It contains a numbered guide to important buildings and street names in the margin.

(7) **Compressed ARC (Equal ARC Second Raster Chart/Map) Digitized Raster Graphic.** Used in any application requiring rapid display of map image or manipulation of the image of a map in raster form.

(8) **Mission-Specific Data Set.** Include planning and reference maps, precise orthorectified image datasets, gridded products, image city maps (ICMs)/graphics and photomaps, digital feature data, NGA point targets, and hard and deeply buried targets.

(9) **Tactical Terrain Data (TTD).** Provides terrain information that is critical to planning and executing joint operations including CAS missions, amphibious operations, and land combat operations. TTD supports such diverse tasks as terrain visualization, mobility, countermobility planning, site and route selection, reconnaissance planning, communications planning, navigation, and munitions guidance.

(10) **World Mean Elevation Data.** A database of minimum, maximum, and mean terrain elevations. The preferred source is DTED. In areas with no DTED coverage, the best medium or small-scale cartographic source is used. Data collected for each 12 by 18 nautical mile cell include minimum and maximum elevation value, arithmetic mean elevation, standard deviation, source, and absolute vertical accuracy.

(11) **World Vector Shoreline Plus.** A digital data file containing the shorelines, international boundaries, and country names of the world. These geographic features are required for many of the digital databases being used to support geographic information systems and weapons systems.

(12) **Image City Maps (ICMs).** Scanned images in Joint Photographic Experts Group and Portable Document Format of paper ICM products at various scales from 1:5,000 to 1:35,000.

(13) **Geospatial-Intelligence Contingency Packages.** A collection of products providing coverage over specific areas designated as evacuation sites by both the Department of State and/or the unified commands.

11. Annex N, Space Operations

Annex N provides a description of weather satellites and weather satellite terminals available to the AOR, along with a brief description of the capabilities these terminals provide. It mentions types (e.g., solar, ionospheric, and geomagnetic disturbances) and levels of possible degradation to communications, radar, and navigation systems which cause mission impacts. Commanders may require specific quantification of impacts at execution; this level of detail will be facilitated as METOC capabilities mature. Optimally, this requires the SMO, JMO, and component METOC forces to be proactive on behalf of their customers in assessing space impacts.

12. Annex P, Host-Nation Support

Annex P should document host nation-provided METOC services and other host-nation support required.

13. Annex R, Reports

Annex R should specify what reports are submitted by METOC elements, communications functions supporting METOC operations, and staff functions about METOC impacts (including space) on operations. In addition, the SMO/JMO should be included as addressees on reports regarding METOC personnel or factors.

14. Annex V, Interagency Coordination

Annex V should specify procedures for coordinating METOC operations or requirements outside of DOD. This may include, but is not limited to, leveraging host nation capabilities (see annex P), other governmental organizations, or NGOs.

APPENDIX D
LOCATION IDENTIFIERS

1. Overview

METOC forces are tasked with providing terrestrial and space environmental information to joint air, land, maritime, space, and SOF, enabling decision makers to correctly evaluate and select appropriate COAs or weapons/platform employment. METOC forces generate time-critical information at all levels of operations in classified or unclassified environments from permanent and temporary locations. To ensure dissemination and sharing of this information, each location originating decodable weather messages requires a site-specific location identifier. For non-permanent locations, METOC forces normally employ a four-letter tactical location identifier (KQ ID) to uniquely identify their site. Note: IDs are used for nonpermanent locations supporting NATO forces; however, they are managed by Germany's Bundeswehr Geoinformation Office.

2. Management of Tactical Location Identifiers

a. The Air Force is the designated DOD executive agent for the KQ ID process. The Air Force has in turn designated HQ AFWA as the lead agent to accomplish KQ ID management.

b. KQ IDs are typically assigned to METOC forces:

    (1) Deployed to support exercises or real-world contingencies.

    (2) Supporting garrison training or exercises in the immediate operating area of METOC forces or civilian weather stations using permanent International Civil Aviation Organization (ICAO) location identifiers.

    (3) Supporting testing programs requiring temporary location identifiers.

    (4) Denied or pending approval of a requested permanent ICAO/World Meteorological Organization (WMO) location identifier.

    (5) Operating in locations in which the host nation prohibits the use of indigenous ICAO/WMO location identifiers for foreign military operations or in which it was not possible to acquire an approved ICAO/WMO location identifier for the site.

c. **Security Classification.** SMOs/JMOs and Service component METOC forces should refer to the classification guidance for the JTF being supported to determine the appropriate level of classification for the KQ ID. When using a KQ ID, METOC information is unclassified and can be transmitted using unclassified communications means. However, the means of acquiring the data or the location of the data collection may be classified when tied to a sensitive operation. Unclassified systems (e.g., nonsecure telephone or e-mail) shall not be used to correlate a KQ ID to a classified location/operation. Doing so constitutes a breach of security and may compromise military operations. Any breach of security involving KQ IDs shall be reported to the SMO/JMO or, if a JTF is not stood up, to the lead METOC element.

d. The SMO/JMO should serve as the focal point to obtain KQ IDs for the entire JTF, as part of the overall collection plan. As the lead agency for KQ ID management; HQ AFWA will publish KQ ID management policies on an AFWA web site. Specifically, the SMO/JMO should:

(1) Request KQ IDs as far in advance as possible from AFWA's 2nd Weather Group.

(2) Inventory and revalidate subordinate units' KQ ID requirements periodically.

(3) Notify HQ AFWA when KQ IDs are no longer needed and recommend inactivation.

(4) Immediately respond to mitigate compromised KQ IDs. All affected organizations will follow the guidance in DOD Manual 5200.01, Information Security Program: Overview, Classification, and Declassification.

(5) Deconflict KQ IDs in the JTF JOA as required.

(6) Coordinate with HQ AFWA to maintain database and archive METOC information generated under KQ IDs.

e. When a JTF is not stood up, KQ ID requests should normally flow through the Air Force lead METOC element (typically the major command weather functional manager), the Navy lead METOC element for KQ ID requests (typically the Fleet Numerical Meteorology and Oceanography Center), or the Marine Corps lead element (typically the Marine expeditionary force staff weather officer).

f. **Release for Civilian Use.** It is often necessary or prudent to release METOC data and station information associated with unclassified KQ IDs to contractors supporting military operations and other non-DOD organizations. Non-DOD organizations may retrieve observations and forecasts using their organic systems, or they can access the text data from the Aviation Digital Data Service website: http://adds.aviationweather.gov.

APPENDIX E
METEOROLOGICAL AND OCEANOGRAPHIC IMPACTS ON OPERATIONS

"We drew up a list of every natural and geographic handicap—and Inchon had 'em all."

Lieutenant Commander Arlie G. Capps, Gunnery Officer for Task Force 90 at Inchon Landing, September 1950

1. Mission planners and operators must be aware of METOC factors that affect operations, ensuring the greatest chance of mission success. JFCs must be familiar with critical METOC thresholds to effectively employ weapon systems and to provide maximum safety for friendly personnel. Commanders, operators, and planners must communicate their mission-specific thresholds to METOC personnel so that assessments of potential operational impacts can be developed and accurate, relevant, and timely information provided to decision makers during mission planning and execution. METOC personnel must be knowledgeable about critical METOC thresholds for the weapon systems they support, to ensure they provide important information required by decision makers.

2. **Decision Aids.** METOC forces produce decision aids, impacts-matrices (e.g., stoplight charts), and target-area depictions normally through the application of parameter thresholds. These products enable the decision makers to easily relate METOC forecasts with mission, system, and platform thresholds. Increasingly, decision makers extract mission-specific information tailored to their requirements from these netcentric databases.

3. In addition to manual methods for analyzing METOC effects on operations, there are systems that can automatically assess METOC effects. Two examples of these decision aids include Integrated Weather Effects Decision Aid and Target Acquisition Weapons Software. These systems are applicable to both the mission planning and mission execution processes.

4. Weather impacts to systems and operations are typically provided in "stoplight" format with the following criteria:

    a. Green   (Favorable) zero or minimal operational impact.

    b. Amber   (Marginal) moderate operational impact.

    c. Red   (Unfavorable) severe operational impact.

Intentionally Blank

APPENDIX F
METEOROLOGICAL AND OCEANOGRAPHIC INTEGRATION TO JOINT SPECIAL OPERATIONS PLANNING

1. Overview

Joint SO differ from conventional operations in degree of physical and political risk, operational techniques, modes of employment, and dependence on detailed operational intelligence and indigenous assets. These SO require detailed planning. Consequently, intelligence and weather requirements are normally greater in scope and depth than those of conventional forces. SOF's ability to leverage a combination of air, ground, maritime, and space capabilities is significantly affected by adverse environmental conditions which are based on specific environmental sensitivity thresholds inherent to these capabilities.

2. METOC Support to Joint Special Operations Planning

a. Environmental effects should be integrated into JOPP, JIPOE, C2 systems, and the COP. Terrain and weather are natural conditions that profoundly influence operations and favor those better prepared to operate in the environment. Commanders leverage environmental effects/impacts information to select favorable windows of opportunity to execute, support, and sustain specific SOF operations. Operational decisions may be based on exploiting specific environmental conditions to provide the best advantage to friendly forces in comparison to the impact of similar environmental conditions on adversary capabilities. SO commanders' rely on METOC personnel to provide accurate, relevant, timely, and consistent weather information/effects to gain environmental situational awareness, achieve information superiority, fully exploit the asymmetrical environmental advantage necessary to apply and maximize combat power at critical points in space and time and create the desired effects on the battlefield.

b. Within the JIPOE process, METOC personnel develop environmental staff estimates which include an assessment of environmental effects on mission profiles and capabilities under consideration in JOPP. This includes environmental effects on enemy capabilities, weapon systems and mission profiles for possible/potential enemy COAs. These estimates enable commanders and their staffs to visualize the full extent of the operational environment (enemy, weather, and terrain) and to support the commander's situational understanding of the environment and influence decision making. Due to the dynamic nature of SO, environmental running estimates are continuously updated as operational and intelligence details and environmental conditions change.

c. SO commanders also rely on METOC personnel to identify points, routes, and AOR which may be specifically vulnerable to environmental impacts (environmental choke points) which influences the development of environmental CCIRs. SOF commanders rely on weather personnel to make recommendations for the execution of environmental reconnaissance. Commanders may then direct SO weather team personnel to conduct environmental reconnaissance operations, to collect against those CCIRs.

d. METOC personnel can make especially critical inputs during several key phases of JOPP. During the COA development phase of JOPP, SOF commanders expect METOC personnel to provide operationally relevant environmental estimates, based on critical weather thresholds to assess feasibility of mission; anticipate effectiveness of platform, weapon systems and munitions; identify opportunities to exploit environmental conditions for operational advantage; and determine optimal or favorable weather windows of opportunity for conducting operations. During COA analysis and wargaming, METOC personnel identify advantages and disadvantages of each COA based on their environmental estimate which includes an assessment of environmental impacts on the adversary's capabilities in comparison to those of friendly forces. During COA comparison and approval, the environmental estimate is then used in COA comparison to influence the recommended COA and selection rationale. SOF commanders evaluate merits of each COA for environmental and other operational criteria and select a COA.

APPENDIX G
REFERENCES

The development of JP 3-59 is based upon the following primary references:

1. Department of Defense Publication

a. DOD Manual 5200.01, *Information Security Program: Overview, Classification, and Declassification*, Volume 1.

b. DOD Directive 3025.18, *Defense Support of Civil Authorities (DSCA)*.

2. Chairman of the Joint Chiefs of Staff Publications

a. CJCSI 3810.01C, *Meteorological and Oceanographic Operations*.

b. CJCSM 3122.03C, *Joint Operation Planning and Execution System (JOPES) Volume II: Planning Formats*.

c. CJCSM 3500.03C, *Joint Training Manual for the Armed Forces of the United States*.

d. CJCSM 3500.05, *Joint Task Force Headquarters Master Training Guide*.

e. JP 1, *Doctrine for the Armed Forces of the United States*.

f. JP 1-02, *DOD Dictionary of Military and Associated Terms*.

g. JP 2-0, *Joint Intelligence*.

h. JP 2-01.3, *Joint Intelligence Preparation of the Operational Environment*.

i. JP 2-03, *Geospatial Intelligence Support to Joint Operations*.

j. JP 3-0, *Joint Operations*.

k. JP 3-05, *Special Operations*.

l. JP 3-11, *Operations in Chemical, Biological, Radiological, and Nuclear (CBRN) Environments*.

m. JP 3-16, *Multinational Operations*.

n. JP 3-27, *Homeland Defense*.

o. JP 3-28, *Defense Support of Civil Authorities*.

p. JP 3-29, *Foreign Humanitarian Assistance*.

q. JP 3-41, *Chemical, Biological, Radiological, and Nuclear Consequence Management*.

r. JP 5-0, *Joint Operation Planning*.

s. JP 6-0, *Joint Communications System*.

3. Service and Combatant Command Publications

a. Air Force Doctrine Document 3-59, *Weather Operations*.

b. Field Manual (FM) 3-09.15, *Tactics, Techniques, and Procedures for Field Artillery Meteorology*.

c. FM 34-81, *Weather Support for Army Tactical Operations*.

d. FM 2-01.3, *Intelligence Preparation of the Battlefield*.

e. AR 115-10/AFI 15-157 (IP), *Weather Support for the US Army*.

f. Commander, Naval Meteorology and Oceanography Command Instruction 3140.1, *US Navy Meteorological and Oceanographic Support Manual*.

g. Navy Meteorology and Oceanography Command Instruction 1500.3, *Procedures for Qualification and Certification of Navy and Marine Corps Air Traffic Controllers as Tower Visibility Observers*.

h. Marine Corps Warfighting Publication 3-35.7, *MAGTF METOC Support*.

i. Marine Corps Order 6200.1, *Marine Corps Heat Injury Prevention Program*.

j. United States Special Operations Command Manual 525-6, *Critical METOC Thresholds for SOF Operations*.

k. Joint Meteorology and Oceanography (METOC) Handbook.

4. North Atlantic Treaty Organization (NATO) Publications

a. Allied Joint Publication 3.11, *Allied Doctrine for Meteorological and Oceanographic Support to Joint Forces*.

b. NATO MCM-0178-2005, *Integrated METOC Support Concept (IMETOC)*.

5. Other Publications

Geospatial Intelligence (GEOINT) Basic Doctrine Publication 1.

APPENDIX H
ADMINISTRATIVE INSTRUCTIONS

1. User Comments

Users in the field are highly encouraged to submit comments on this publication to: Joint Staff Directorate for Joint Force Development (J-7), Joint Education and Doctrine Division (JEDD), Pentagon Room 2D763, Washington, DC, 20318-7000. These comments should address content (accuracy, usefulness, consistency, and organization), writing, and appearance.

2. Authorship

The lead agent for this publication is the US Air Force. The Joint Staff doctrine sponsor for this publication is the Director for Operations (J-3).

3. Supersession

This publication supersedes JP 3-59, 24 September 2008, *Meteorological and Oceanographic Operations.*

4. Change Recommendations

a. Recommendations for urgent changes to this publication should be submitted:

TO: JOINT STAFF WASHINGTON DC//J7-JEDD//

b. Routine changes should be submitted electronically to the Deputy Director, Joint Staff J-7, Joint and Coalition Warfighting/Joint Doctrine Support Division and info the lead agent and the Director for Joint Force Development, J-7/JEDD.

c. When a Joint Staff directorate submits a proposal to the CJCS that would change source document information reflected in this publication, that directorate will include a proposed change to this publication as an enclosure to its proposal. The Services and other organizations are requested to notify the Joint Staff J-7 when changes to source documents reflected in this publication are initiated.

5. Distribution of Publications

Local reproduction is authorized, and access to unclassified publications is unrestricted. However, access to, and reproduction authorization for, classified joint publications must be in accordance with DOD Manual 5200.01, Volume 1, *DOD Information Security Program: Overview, Classification, and Declassification,* and DOD Manual 5200.01, Volume 3, *DOD Information Security Program: Protection of Classified Information.*

6. Distribution of Electronic Publications

a. Joint Staff J-7 will not print copies of JPs for distribution. Electronic versions are available on JDEIS at https://jdeis.js.mil (NIPRNET) and http://jdeis.js.smil.mil (SIPRNET), and on the JEL at http://www.dtic.mil/doctrine (NIPRNET).

b. Only approved JPs and joint test publications are releasable outside the CCMDs, Services, and Joint Staff. Release of any classified JP to foreign governments or foreign nationals must be requested through the local embassy (Defense Attaché Office) to Defense Intelligence Agency (DIA), Defense Foreign Liaison/IE-3, 200 MacDill Blvd., Joint Base Anacostia-Bolling, Washington, DC 20340-5100.

c. JEL CD-ROM. Upon request of a joint doctrine development community member, the Joint Staff J-7 will produce and deliver one CD-ROM with current JPs. This JEL CD-ROM will be updated not less than semi-annually and when received can be locally reproduced for use within the CCMDs and Services.

GLOSSARY
PART I—ABBREVIATIONS AND ACRONYMS

ADCON	administrative control
ADP	automated data processing
AFFOR	Air Force forces
AFI	Air Force instruction
AFWA	Air Force Weather Agency
ANG	Air National Guard
AOI	area of interest
AOR	area of responsibility
AR	Army regulation
ARFOR	Army forces
ARTYMET	artillery meteorological
ATC	air traffic control
BCT	brigade combat team
BT	bathythermograph
C2	command and control
CAS	close air support
CBRN	chemical, biological, radiological, and nuclear
CCDR	combatant commander
CCIR	commander's critical information requirement
CCMD	combatant command
CD-ROM	compact disk read-only memory
CIB	controlled image base
CJCS	Chairman of the Joint Chiefs of Staff
CJCSI	Chairman of the Joint Chiefs of Staff instruction
CJCSM	Chairman of the Joint Chiefs of Staff manual
CJTF	commander, joint task force
CNM	classified notice to mariners
COA	course of action
CONOPS	concept of operations
CONPLAN	concept plan
COP	common operational picture
DBDB-V	digital bathymetric database variable
DHS	Department of Homeland Security
DNC	digital nautical chart
DOD	Department of Defense
DSCA	defense support of civil authorities
DTED	digital terrain elevation data
DTRA	Defense Threat Reduction Agency

FALOP	Forward Area Limited Observing Program
FM	field manual (Army)
G-2	Army or Marine Corps component intelligence staff officer (Army division or higher staff, Marine Corps brigade or higher staff)
GBS	Global Broadcast System
GCC	geographic combatant commander
GEOINT	geospatial intelligence
GI&S	geospatial information and services
HQ	headquarters
IAW	in accordance with
ICAO	International Civil Aviation Organization
ICM	image city map
IMAAC	Interagency Modeling and Atmospheric Assessment Center
J-6	communications system directorate of a joint staff
JFC	joint force commander
JIPOE	joint intelligence preparation of the operational environment
JMCC	joint meteorological and oceanographic coordination cell
JMCO	joint meteorological and oceanographic coordination organization
JMO	joint meteorological and oceanographic officer
JOA	joint operations area
JOAF	joint operations area forecast
JOPES	Joint Operation Planning and Execution System
JOPP	joint operation planning process
JP	joint publication
JRSOI	joint reception, staging, onward movement, and integration
JTF	joint task force
KQ ID	tactical location identifier
MACS	Marine air control squadron
MAGTF	Marine air-ground task force
MARFOR	Marine Corps forces
METOC	meteorological and oceanographic
MNFC	multinational force commander
MOP	measure of performance
MOSC	meteorological and oceanographic operations support community
N-2	Navy component intelligence staff officer
NATO	North Atlantic Treaty Organization

NAVFOR	Navy forces
NGA	National Geospatial-Intelligence Agency
NGO	nongovernmental organization
NIPRNET	Nonsecure Internet Protocol Router Network
NOAA	National Oceanic and Atmospheric Administration
NTM	notice to mariners
NWS	National Weather Service
OAI	oceanographic area of interest
OPCON	operational control
OPLAN	operation plan
OPORD	operation order
OPSEC	operations security
OWS	operational weather squadron
PIREP	pilot report
S-2	battalion or brigade intelligence staff officer (Army; Marine Corps battalion or regiment)
SIPRNET	SECRET Internet Protocol Router Network
SMO	senior meteorological and oceanographic officer
SO	special operations
SOF	special operations forces
TOD	tactical ocean data
TPFDD	time-phased force and deployment data
TTD	tactical terrain data
TTP	tactics, techniques, and procedures
UAS	unmanned aircraft system
USC	United States Code
USG	United States Government
USNO	United States Naval Observatory
USTRANSCOM	United States Transportation Command
UTC	Coordinated Universal Time
VMap	vector map
WAI	weather area of interest
WBGTI	wet bulb globe temperature index
WMO	World Meteorological Organization

PART II—TERMS AND DEFINITIONS

atmospheric environment. The envelope of air surrounding the Earth, including its interfaces and interactions with the Earth's solid or liquid surface. (JP 1-02. SOURCE: JP 3-59)

joint meteorological and oceanographic coordination cell. A subset of a joint meteorological and oceanographic coordination organization, which is delegated the responsibility of executing the coordination of meteorological and oceanographic support operations in the operational area. Also called JMCC. (Approved for incorporation into JP 1-02.)

joint meteorological and oceanographic coordination organization. A Service meteorological and oceanographic organization that is designated within the operations order as the lead organization responsible for coordinating meteorological and oceanographic operations support in the operational area. Also called JMCO. (Approved for incorporation into JP 1-02.)

joint meteorological and oceanographic officer. Officer designated to provide direct meteorological and oceanographic support to a joint force commander. Also called JMO. (JP 1-02. SOURCE: JP 3-59)

joint operations area forecast. The official baseline meteorological and oceanographic forecast for operational planning and mission execution within the joint operations area. Also called JOAF. (JP 1-02. SOURCE: JP 3-59)

maritime environment. None. (Approved for removal from JP 1-02.)

meteorological and oceanographic. A term used to convey all environmental factors, from the sub-bottom of the Earth's oceans through maritime, land areas, airspace, ionosphere, and outward into space. Also called METOC. (Approved for incorporation into JP 1-02.)

meteorological and oceanographic data. Measurements or observations of meteorological and oceanographic variables. (JP 1-02. SOURCE: JP 3-59)

meteorological and oceanographic environment. The surroundings that extend from the sub-bottom of the Earth's oceans, through maritime, land areas, airspace, ionosphere, and outward into space, which include conditions, resources, and natural phenomena, in and through which the joint force operates. (Approved for incorporation into JP 1-02.)

meteorological and oceanographic information. Actionable information to include meteorological, climatological, oceanographic, and space environment observations, analyses, prognostic data or products and meteorological and oceanographic effects. (Approved for inclusion in JP 1-02.)

meteorological and oceanographic operations support community. The collective of electronically connected, shore-based meteorological and oceanographic production facilities/centers, theater and/or regional meteorological and oceanographic production activities. Also called MOSC. (JP 1-02. SOURCE: JP 3-59)

meteorological watch. Monitoring the weather for a route, area, or terminal and advising concerned organizations when hazardous conditions that could affect their operations or pose a hazard to life or property are observed or forecast to occur. Also called METWATCH. (Approved for inclusion in JP 1-02.)

meteorology. The study dealing with the phenomena of the atmosphere including the physics, chemistry, and dynamics extending to the effects of the atmosphere on the Earth's surface and the oceans. (JP 1-02. SOURCE: JP 3-59)

oceanography. The study of the sea, embracing and integrating all knowledge pertaining to the sea and its physical boundaries, the chemistry and physics of seawater, and marine biology. (Approved for incorporation into JP 1-02.)

precise time and time interval. A reference value of time and time interval (frequency). Also called PTTI. (Approved for incorporation into JP 1-02.)

senior meteorological and oceanographic officer. Meteorological and oceanographic officer responsible for assisting the combatant commander and staff in developing and executing operational meteorological and oceanographic service concepts in support of a designated joint force. Also called SMO. (JP 1-02. SOURCE: JP 3-59)

space environment. The environment corresponding to the space domain, where electromagnetic radiation, charged particles, and electric and magnetic fields are the dominant physical influences, and that encompasses the earth's ionosphere and magnetosphere, interplanetary space, and the solar atmosphere. (JP 1-02. SOURCE: JP 3-59)

space weather. The conditions and phenomena in space and specifically in the near-Earth environment that may affect space assets or space operations. (Approved for incorporation into JP 1-02.)

terrestrial environment. The Earth's land area, including its man-made and natural surface and sub-surface features, and its interfaces and interactions with the atmosphere and the oceans. (Approved for incorporation into JP 1-02 with JP 3-59 as the source JP.)

Intentionally Blank

JOINT DOCTRINE PUBLICATIONS HIERARCHY

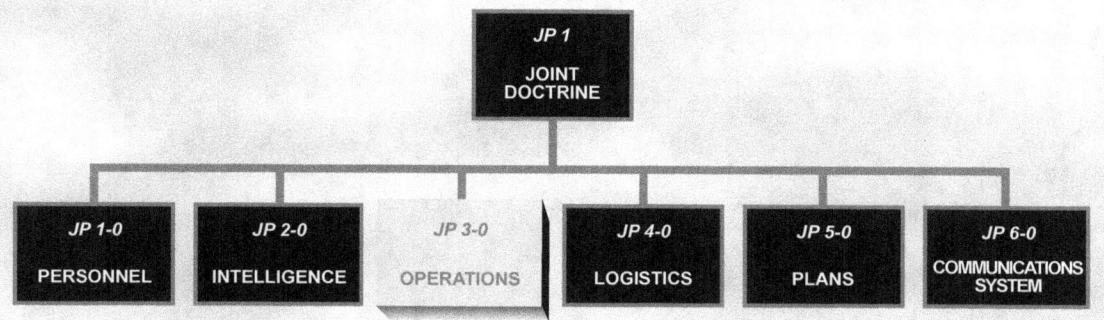

```
                    ┌──────────────┐
                    │     JP 1     │
                    │    JOINT     │
                    │   DOCTRINE   │
                    └──────────────┘
```

JP 1-0	JP 2-0	JP 3-0	JP 4-0	JP 5-0	JP 6-0
PERSONNEL	INTELLIGENCE	OPERATIONS	LOGISTICS	PLANS	COMMUNICATIONS SYSTEM

All joint publications are organized into a comprehensive hierarchy as shown in the chart above. **Joint Publication (JP) 3-59** is in the **Operations** series of joint doctrine publications. The diagram below illustrates an overview of the development process:

STEP #4 - Maintenance

- JP published and continuously assessed by users
- Formal assessment begins 24 27 months following publication
- Revision begins 3.5 years after publication
- Each JP revision is completed no later than 5 years after signature

STEP #1 - Initiation

- Joint doctrine development community (JDDC) submission to fill extant operational void
- Joint Staff (JS) J 7 conducts front end analysis
- Joint Doctrine Planning Conference validation
- Program directive (PD) development and staffing/joint working group
- PD includes scope, references, outline, milestones, and draft authorship
- JS J 7 approves and releases PD to lead agent (LA) (Service, combatant command, JS directorate)

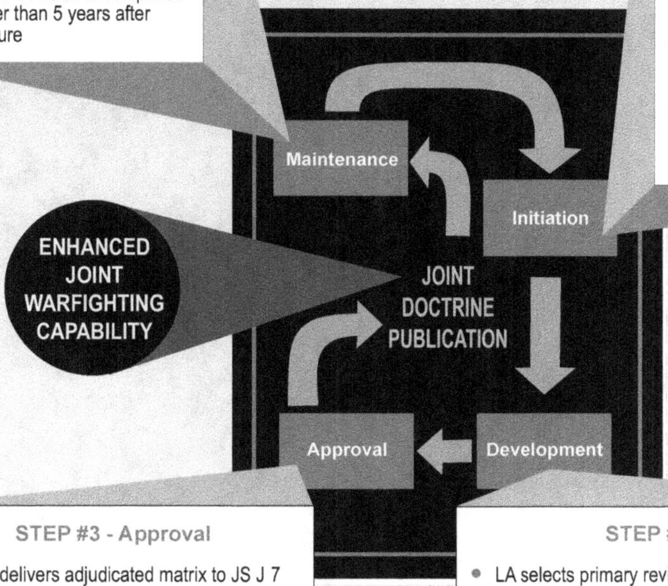

ENHANCED JOINT WARFIGHTING CAPABILITY

Maintenance → Initiation → JOINT DOCTRINE PUBLICATION → Development → Approval

STEP #3 - Approval

- JSDS delivers adjudicated matrix to JS J 7
- JS J 7 prepares publication for signature
- JSDS prepares JS staffing package
- JSDS staffs the publication via JSAP for signature

STEP #2 - Development

- LA selects primary review authority (PRA) to develop the first draft (FD)
- PRA develops FD for staffing with JDDC
- FD comment matrix adjudication
- JS J 7 produces the final coordination (FC) draft, staffs to JDDC and JS via Joint Staff Action Processing (JSAP) system
- Joint Staff doctrine sponsor (JSDS) adjudicates FC comment matrix
- FC joint working group